Tilting Education

Do you sometimes wonder what you and your school stand for? Have you ever felt that important issues lurk beneath the surface, but you lack the capacity to bring them into focus? *Tilting Education* will inspire, challenge, and empower those who want to help lead a quiet revolution in schools. The book examines some of the most interesting ideas found in psychology, philosophy, sport, the arts, and economics to raise fundamental questions about what lessons we should want young people to learn and how these lessons could best be taught.

Setting out a model for developing more sustainable and kinder schools, the book focuses on a range of issues such as value and success, effective planning, the sensible use of data, staff training and motivation, communication, diversity, and ethics. Each chapter encourages the reader to think deeply about their priorities for education and provides practical strategies that will motivate staff, reduce workload pressure, and improve learning and teaching.

Imaginative and creative leaders of academic, pastoral, and senior teams will gain insights and tips from *Tilting Education* to rebalance the perception of educational value in their schools. More than a check list of dos and do nots, this is a book that will change the way you think about your school. It will inspire and support you to make it a better place, which will serve your whole school community with kindness, into the future.

Jo Clemmet has taught and led in schools across the North-West and East Midlands of England for the last twenty-five years, and recently at the University of Nottingham. He lives in Beeston with his wonderful wife and four fabulous children.

Tilting Education

Rebalancing Schools to Create Success That Is Kind for Students and Staff

Jo Clemmet

LONDON AND NEW YORK

Cover image: © Getty Images

First published 2023
by Routledge
4 Park Square, Milton Park, Abingdon, Oxon OX14 4RN

and by Routledge
605 Third Avenue, New York, NY 10158

Routledge is an imprint of the Taylor & Francis Group, an informa business

© 2023 Jo Clemmet

The right of Jo Clemmet to be identified as author of this work has been asserted in accordance with sections 77 and 78 of the Copyright, Designs and Patents Act 1988.

All rights reserved. No part of this book may be reprinted or reproduced or utilised in any form or by any electronic, mechanical, or other means, now known or hereafter invented, including photocopying and recording, or in any information storage or retrieval system, without permission in writing from the publishers.

Trademark notice: Product or corporate names may be trademarks or registered trademarks, and are used only for identification and explanation without intent to infringe.

British Library Cataloguing-in-Publication Data
A catalogue record for this book is available from the British Library

Library of Congress Cataloging-in-Publication Data
Names: Clemmet, Jo, author.
Title: Tilting education: rebalancing schools to create success that is kind for students and staff / Jo Clemmet.
Description: First Edition. | New York: Routledge, 2023. | Includes bibliographical references and index.
Identifiers: LCCN 2022022363 | ISBN 9781032148748 (Hardback) | ISBN 9781032148786 (Paperback) | ISBN 9781003241546 (eBook)
Subjects: LCSH: Educational sociology. | Educational change. | School improvement programs. | Educational leadership.
Classification: LCC LC191 .C5385 2023 | DDC 306.43—dc23/eng/20220713
LC record available at https://lccn.loc.gov/2022022363

ISBN: 978-1-032-14874-8 (hbk)
ISBN: 978-1-032-14878-6 (pbk)
ISBN: 978-1-003-24154-6 (ebk)

DOI: 10.4324/9781003241546

Typeset in Melior
by codeMantra

For Claire, without whom I am not me.

Contents

List of Figures ix
List of Tables xi

Introduction 1

1 Tilting values 4

2 Tilting models 18

3 Tilting evidence 35

4 Tilting teams 54

5 Tilting commitment 70

6 Tilting problems 87

7 Tilting leadership 105

Conclusion 122

Bibliography 127
Index 129

Figures

1.1	Pessimistic future view	15
1.2	Optimistic future view	15
2.1	The curve symbol	21
2.2	The doughnut school model	28
2.3	Dividing the doughnut	29
2.4	Ceilings and floors	33
4.1	Division of labour	56
4.2	Team diversity	59
4.3	Team skills and thinking diversity	60
4.4	TILT team vs. clone team	61
4.5	The shape of a leader	64
4.6	T-shaped TILT team	67
5.1	Evolving TILT teams	72
5.2	Motivation and commitment	75
5.3	Performance curve	80
5.4	Maslow's hierarchy of needs	81
6.1	Sanctum syndrome	97
6.2	Making the unseen, seen (1)	101
6.3	Making the unseen, seen (2)	102
8.1	Overton's window	123

Tables

1.1	Identifying personal values	5
1.2	Jotham's story	6
1.3	Identifying shared values	8
1.4	The future of values	16
2.1	Thought experiment	19
2.2	The power of symbols	20
2.3	The map is not the territory	24
2.4	Incommensurate and conflicting goals	27
2.5	Setting goals	30
2.6	Setting success ranges	32
3.1	Top 10 TV programmes of 202021	37
3.2	What evidence do you regularly collect in school?	39
3.3	Principal/agent problems	42
3.4	What evidence should we collect?	44
3.5	What is wrong with that?	47
3.6	Is praise an effective motivator?	51
3.7	Avoiding errors	52
4.1	Division of labour	56
4.2	Team diversity	61
4.3	Is dominance ever right?	62
4.4	T-shaped teams	67
5.1	Inspiring motivation	71
5.2	Returning to motivation	74
5.3	Developing epoché	76
5.4	Giving and receiving feedback	79
5.5	How useful are your lesson observations?	82
5.6	Make a plan	85
6.1	Big ideas in education	88
6.2	Moral algebra and Franklin's gambit	92
6.3	Incompletely theorised agreements	93

6.4	Pre-mortems – If we can predict it, we can prevent it	95
6.5	What are the misbehaviours?	98
6.6	Fun with nudging	102
7.1	Hedgehog or fox? (1)	106
7.2	Hedgehog or fox? (2)	108
7.3	Hedgehog or fox? (3)	109
7.4	Trouble ahead	112
7.5	Taking distinctive action	115
7.6	Judgement by numbers	116
7.7	Truth or dare	117
7.8	Your non-negotiables	120

Tables

1.1	Values, goals, and actions	9
1.2	Values and proxy measures	12
2.1	Doughnut development planning	32

Introduction

Anyone who has been involved in schools, for even a short period of time, will know they are vibrant and dynamic places. They are also stressful. There is little time for review or discussion. The emphasis is on efficiency and getting things done.

Education is full of good people facing difficult issues, but with little time or energy to investigate the credentials of possible solutions. The result is a susceptibility to gimmicks and fads. As we grasp at solutions, one approach after another achieves supremacy before being discredited and falling by the wayside. The vacuum is quickly filled by the next big idea and so the cycle continues.

This book is a call for educators to slow down, look around, and take in fresh views. To reassess priorities by looking at education from different angles. We must not be insular; there is a lot to learn from the world outside.

Creating change should be "the art of looking at what we already know with different eyes, and asking different questions".[i] *Tilting Education* helps teachers do this by borrowing smart ideas from psychology, economics, sport, and philosophy. Its aim is to inspire, challenge, and empower all those in education to create sustainable success which is kind to students and staff. Although teachers do not have a monopoly on common sense, we do have credibility built on hours of lived experience of schools. We all therefore have a part to play in engaging with the big issues and embodying the changes we want to see. Our voice needs to be heard more loudly, and this book aims to provide a shared vocabulary with which to challenge the status quo.

The logic of a league table

The early chapters of the book question the power of competition to improve schools. In the last thirty years, competitive thinking has seeped into a whole range of fields. From waiting times in healthcare to audience figures in the arts, schools are not alone in being asked to focus on the measurable above the valuable. Economic, competitive thinking in non-economic settings is often referred to as 'marketisation' and it began to dominate the UK education scene in the early 1990s, where it stubbornly remains to this day. Characterised by progress measures and league tables, marketisation can fuel an obsession with targets and results, leading to high-stakes, binary judgements of success or failure.

There is a beguilingly simplistic logic to league tables; however, they belong to a former era. This book will examine alternative ways of thinking which are fit for the problems we face in a globalised world of climate crisis and advanced technology. The ideas discussed in these early chapters look at why the logic of league tables has persisted. It goes on to provide theories, practical strategies, and training resources, to question the established consensus, which is doing school students and staff so much harm.

Ironically, the concepts of marketisation and competition came from mainstream economics, but economics has changed significantly in the interim. The uncritical faith in free markets has been challenged by a more nuanced approach which acknowledges goals which are less tangible than profit and loss. This book will argue that education needs to move on too, and will advocate new ways to think about true value in education and how success should be judged.

Teams and commitment

Successful organisations harness the power of diversity in their thinking. Effective teams in politics, sport, and business thrive when colleagues with differing expertise respect each other enough to openly disagree. Diverse views are aired, and discussion is encouraged. The middle chapters will help you to think about how you can ensure diversity of ideas in your teams and inspire maximum commitment from the colleagues you lead and work alongside. Unlike in sport, in education there is no transfer market. Instead, we must work together to evolve and improve.

Strong relationships build genuine commitment, immune to changing circumstances. The middle chapters will look at how teachers can be freed to build authentic relationships and express themselves in the classroom. This requires strategies to challenge debatable theories, sometimes disguised as evidence-based practice. It also involves remodelling leadership hierarchies which rely on dominance for control. Too often schools are bedevilled by the weight of expectation and the threat of judgement, which drain creativity. Humans instead succeed when they are unencumbered by theory and liberated to act on reliable instincts, honed by experience.

The book argues that more thought should be given to addressing the emotional causes of stress for students and staff. Providing practical strategies for coping should run alongside well-meaning programmes to protect well-being. Accepting that dangerous stress is inevitable makes it a self-fulfilling prophecy. Schools instead need to work towards eliminating dangerous stress, not just treating its symptoms.

The final chapters focus on the best ways for leaders to develop strategies to face the unique challenges schools face. Too often schools search for magic bullet solutions which are then pursued doggedly at great cost to staff and student mental health. Sometimes, however, the best way to approach an issue is sideways, thinking laterally and not being too proud to admit when a change of course is required.

Changing minds

There is a danger that we are so accustomed to the dominant educational culture, we are blind to the dangers it poses. Society is undergoing a period of profound upheaval which presents opportunities for change, as well as multiple challenges. We must be careful not to slip back into comfortable, bad habits, once the storms pass.

All of us who care about education have the responsibility to be outward looking and take lessons from wherever they can be found. We also need to be confident, as experts in education, to interpret these ideas and shape debate about education for the future. This book adapts ideas about values, success, modelling, the use of data, commitment, problem solving, and leadership. It will challenge you to reflect on your experiences and beliefs and give suggestions for catalysing change in your school, regardless of your current role.

More than a checklist of dos and do nots, this is a book which will change the way you think about your school. It will inspire and support you to make it a better place, which will serve your whole school community well into the future. Written by a serving school leader who continues to teach and lead full time in comprehensive education, it contains multiple ideas for training activities which can be lifted straight from the book, combined, and used to build bespoke CPD sessions.

For too long educational debate has centred around how to improve a narrow range of statistical outcomes. Brilliant and caring leaders with sharp intellects concentrate more on finessing the system than looking for possibilities beyond it. This book is designed to challenge established thinking and reenergise your passion for what truly matters in education.

Reference

i   Ngugi wa Thiong'o, 2007. *Wizard of the crow*. Random House.

'TILT' meanings

1. **TILT** – adjusting the angle of an image to give a new perspective.
2. **TILT** – a slight change in the incline of a surface to overcome inertia, e.g. the tilting of a table football table to set a becalmed ball back in motion.

Each chapter outlines ideas designed to open new perspectives. They are interspersed by 'Tilting the table' sections which outline practical strategies to overcoming inertia and help change happen in your school.

Tilting values

If you ask a group of teachers to identify the key features that would characterise a successful student when they leave school, the answers are revealing. Invariably they first identify values such as kindness, confidence, and perseverance. Achievements, including exam grades, tend to come later. Yet, we have an education system which often relegates values to a secondary concern or even a naive indulgence: is this madness?

This chapter will start by considering where personal values come from and ask you to reflect on your own personal values. It will then contrast personal values with shared values and highlight the difficulties that arise when these clash. Next, it will consider the ways that value is measured in education and the perverse incentives this can create to change what we teach and how we teach it. Finally, it will advocate for values to be brought back to the centre of education, highlighting the benefits for students, schools, and society.

Personal values

Personal values influence the way we feel, think, and make choices. We rarely articulate them, but they determine how we spend money, what we do in our spare time, and who our friends are. Most of us are heavily influenced by the values of our immediate family and the society we grow up in, either adopting or reacting against the values we encounter.

Values are made visible by actions. We subconsciously judge the values of others through their behaviour. Do they interrupt when others are speaking? Are they generous with their time? Do they praise others? It is through interaction and discussion that the clearest picture of your own values and those of others emerges; 'How can I know what I think until I see what I say"[1] (Tilting the table 1.1).

Under normal circumstances, your actions will be in harmony with the personal values from which they flow and there would be plenty of evidence to convict you. However, there may be occasions when you experience the mental discomfort of having to act in ways that contradict your personal values. The state of mental

Tilting the table 1.1 Identifying personal values

Take a moment to study the table below and identify the six values you would most like others to identify with you.

Dependability	Open-mindedness	Honesty	Spirit of adventure	Education
Reliability	Creativity	Good humour	Motivation	Service to others
Loyalty	Efficiency	Compassion	Positivity	Environmentalism
Commitment	Innovation	Respect	Optimism	Faith in a higher power
Consistency	Perseverance	Courage	Passion	Fitness
Loving/caring	Learning	Success	Contentment	Looking good
Other	Other	Other	Other	Other

Now ask yourself the question:
If you were taken to court and accused of holding the six personal values you have identified as being most important to you – would there be enough evidence from your professional life to convict you?

discomfort resulting from holding two conflicting beliefs, values, or attitudes is termed 'cognitive dissonance'. We are familiar with cognitive dissonance in soap operas. For example, the anxiety a character feels whilst carrying on an affair, or pilfering money is caused by cognitive dissonance. It is not only fictional, however; it also causes big problems in education.

You may have experienced cognitive dissonance if you have had to follow a behaviour policy with which you disagree or feel under pressure to inflate a test score to hit a target. Maybe you have been told to concentrate your time and energy on supporting one group of students which you feel will be at the expense of another. If the values that brought you into the profession conflict with the behaviours expected of you within the profession, the result is likely to be anxiety and stress.

If you are experiencing cognitive dissonance it needs to be resolved. You must either leave, conform to, or try to change, the values of the workplace. This book advocates for teachers to be given the opportunity to change the values of their school and for all teachers to take on this responsibility. One of the most important personal values we need to develop in schools is leadership at all levels. When all teachers are involved in leading change, values are harmonised, and dissonance is diminished.

Good schools are full of talented people who challenge each other to achieve their best. All teachers are experienced in communicating compelling messages to large groups of people, caring for vulnerable individuals, creating exciting resources, and planning for development in the short, medium, and long term. Good teachers work well under pressure and have high expectations of themselves and others. Being a good teacher means having the skills to be a good leader.

However, the fixed and hierarchical leadership structures in many schools can squash interest and involvement in leading change. Professionals who show flair

Tilting the table 1.2 Jotham's story

Read the following extract and think about the questions underneath. It is told by a character called Jotham. He is the youngest son of a King who has just died. His brothers have all been killed by his ambitious and ruthless half-brother, Abimelech, who is now about to be crowned king. Jotham shouts the parable to the crowd who have gathered for the coronation.

"One day the trees went out to anoint a king for themselves. They said to the olive tree, 'Be our king'.

"But the olive tree answered, 'Should I give up my oil, by which both gods and humans are honoured, to hold sway over the trees?'

"Next, the trees said to the fig tree, 'Come and be our king'.

"But the fig tree replied, 'Should I give up my fruit, so good and sweet, to hold sway over the trees?'

"Then the trees said to the vine, 'Come and be our king'.

"But the vine answered, 'Should I give up my wine, which cheers both gods and humans, to hold sway over the trees?'

"Finally, all the trees said to the thornbush, 'Come and be our king'.

"The thornbush said to the trees, 'If you really want to anoint me king over you, come and take refuge in my shade ...'

Judges 9 v8–15

Potential questions to use with a group:
Who do you think the crowd of 'trees' represent?
Why do you think the olive tree, fig tree, and vine refuse to be king?
Do you think the thornbush will be a good king?
Where do you see yourself in this story?

---

and charisma in the classroom often become mute in meetings of staff. Developing staff who are confident in their abilities and eager to share their talents is a key part of school leadership (Tilting the table 1.2).

Shared responsibility

The ancient middle east, where the story is set, was the first part of the world to develop agriculture. Olive trees, fig trees, and vines were cared for by farmers who would harvest their fruit year after year to feed their families and supply their community. These trees would be well known as symbols of productive fruitfulness. Thornbushes, on the other hand, grew wild. They had sparse leaves and a multitude of long, needle-sharp thorns. Thornbushes produce no fruit.

In the story, the crowd of trees want a leader. First, they approach the fruitful olive tree, fig tree, and vine. Each are good candidates due to their obvious fruitfulness, but each is too busy producing fruit to get involved with leadership. In desperation the crowd ask the thornbush to be their king. Despite its sparse leaves which offer little shade and its thorns which wound the unwary, the trees would rather follow the thorn bush than have to take on leadership themselves.

The crowd of trees just wanted to be led. They rushed from one candidate to another and ended up with a poor and dangerous leader. There is no question of them taking any responsibility.

However, the olive tree, fig tree, and vine were all good candidates to lead. Each was fruitful and fulfilling a valuable role but had no interest in leading. Any one of them could have paused in their endeavours to engage with the crowd and show leadership, but none of them did. They were busy and successful and could have been great leaders. But because of their swift refusals, the trees ended up with a leader who could provide little fruit and potentially cause harm. All the trees suffered.

Schools are full of olive trees, fig trees, and vines. Brilliant teachers whose classrooms are alive with creativity and energy. Dedicated, caring, and creative professionals who lack time and energy for more. Maybe they have been bruised before when they pushed themselves out of their comfort zone, or perhaps they are too self-deprecating to believe they can contribute to wider school leadership. Whatever the reason, it is vital to convince staff their values are important and that they can play a valuable role in leading the school agenda forward.

Thornbushes offer little shade from the harsh sun and cause nasty injuries if not handled carefully. The values we share are too important to leave to somebody else. In the next section, we will look at how shared values are formed and why they are so important in shaping a coherent and caring school.

Shared values

Most of us enjoy a trip to the cinema, but have you ever remained in your seat as the lights come up, watched the credits roll, and wondered why there are so many names on the screen? Literally hundreds of people receive an acknowledgement for their work at the end of the film but exactly what most of them do is a mystery. These people are highly creative and specialised in their spheres but many of them will never meet and their work will spread across many weeks and potentially straddle continents. How is it done?

It is the job of a film director to harness the disparate skills and egos and manage the logistics that unite all the inputs into one coherent artistic endeavour. That is why people like Christopher Nolan, Kathryn Bigelow, and Chloe Zhao are as well-known as they are. The director must communicate an inspiring concept and shared production values that will unite their team. They then rely on having the experts in each department to interpret the values consistently and produce a coherent film. No individual could make a feature film on their own, but the director ensures that the team are unified by shared values that give the impression of one, overriding intent.

Like a film set, a school is a complex organisation with hundreds of people working together to achieve a common goal. Every school needs to share a view of what they are trying to achieve. They also need the best possible people working in every role to challenge each other in search of improvement and great results. In many ways, however, a school is even more complex. Schools do not stop and start; they flow from one year to the next. The rhythm of terms gives shape to the flow and there are new beginnings and endings, but these overlap rather than coinciding. Schools have no script and are never complete in the way a film is.

However, the fact that schools are long-lasting provides an important advantage. Film crews consist of hundreds of freelancers who come together for short periods before everyone moves on to their next project. In schools, the overlaps between staff coming and going allow shared values to take root in the long term, if they are carefully nurtured.

There is a well-known story of President Kennedy visiting NASA headquarters in 1961 and coming across a caretaker sweeping the floor. JFK introduced himself and asked the floor sweeper what he did at NASA. The janitor paused, looked the president in the eye and replied, "I'm helping to put a man on the moon".

Discussing and agreeing the most important values your school stands for can serve as an important motivator and unifier. Keep them simple enough for your pupils to understand and limit them to a maximum of three to aid recall. Provided they are not just words for the wall, sharing values will illuminate your school's ultimate purpose for staff, students, and parents building shared commitment and success.

Unlike personal values, shared values must be actively chosen and agreed. If the people in the organisation have played a part in formulating values, they will know and understand them and, like the cleaner at NASA, be inspired. A valid set of shared values will translate into visible actions, and this is where their power lies for schools (Tilting the table 1.3).

Shared values are the common beliefs that pervade complex organisations such as schools. They define what the school thinks is important. Shared values ensure that multiple goals can be achieved, and myriad actions take place, whilst maintaining consistency of purpose. They enable hundreds of lessons to be taught and thousands of decisions to be taken every day, without consultation, whilst preserving unity of purpose. The next section will look at the link between values and actions in more detail.

Tilting the table 1.3 Identifying shared values

Questions for discussion:

1. What are your school's shared values?
2. How would you like a visitor to your organisation to see these shared values in action? (give practical examples if possible)

Turning shared values into actions

Quiet reigned on the corridors as the head teacher made their way around the school with the Chair of Governors. Passing a classroom door, the pair popped in to see what was going on. The teacher was standing in front of a colourful diagram and when asked, told the head he was, "Teaching about global warming". On entering a second classroom they noticed the same diagram on the board and asked the same question. "I am helping students understand the impact of people on the environment" was the reply. Finally, they entered a third classroom. The students were busily engaged, and the colourful diagram was on the board again. When asked what they were doing, the final teacher replied, "I am developing responsible citizens".

The story is intended to draw out the differences between actions, goals, and values. All three teachers were teaching the same lesson but conceptualising it in very different ways. The first teacher understood what they were doing in terms of actions, teaching a lesson on global warming. The second understood it in terms of contributing to an intermediate goal within the geography curriculum, linking people and environment. The final teacher understood their purpose as consolidating a shared value, developing students who are responsible citizens.

Actions, goals, and values are 'nested' (Table 1.1). You could ask the third teacher how they were developing responsible citizens (value) and they might respond by saying they were teaching about the links between people and the environment (goal). If pushed further, they could respond that they were teaching about the goal by delivering a lesson on global warming (action). If they were parts of a Russian doll, values would be the outer layer, containing goals which, in turn, would contain actions.

In contrast, the first teacher simply conceptualised their lesson as the action of teaching about global warming. There is nothing wrong with this, but it is only a fraction of the ultimate purpose which the school is striving for, as expressed by its shared values.

Teachers who are secure in the shared values of the school will contextualise every goal they set and every action they take in terms of a shared value. Every interaction, lesson taught, or homework marked becomes an opportunity to reinforce kindness, aspiration, responsibility, or another important shared value. If all staff share this approach, the values quickly become embedded, and success follows.

Table 1.1 Values, goals, and actions

		Assessment
Value	Developing responsible citizens	?
Goal	People and the environment	Exam/test result
Actions	Lesson on global warming	Lesson observation/Planning sample

But there is a problem. Values are the ultimate purpose of education, but they can be elusive and hard to quantify. Coming to school every day with the intention of developing responsible citizens or kind students, for example, is important, but what does it mean in practice?

Abstract values cannot be measured. They need to be translated into concrete goals and actions. In teaching, goals are usually expressed in terms of performance measures, such as exam or test results. Meanwhile, actions most commonly take the form of lessons. We therefore measure the output of tests or lessons as a substitute or 'proxy' for the value they represent. It is when these proxies (e.g. test data, exam results, lesson observations) become all we see, and shared values are forgotten, that problems arise.

Prizing the measurable over the valuable

Lessons, lesson plans, and exam results have become the focus of minute attention over the last thirty years for understandable reasons. Lessons are the most visible manifestation of teaching and learning, and they can be captured on paper in the form of a plan. For many years lesson plans were mandatory in many schools and lessons were routinely judged by Office for Standards in Education, Children's Services and Skills (Ofsted) criteria. A couple of understandable assumptions underlie this focus on planning, lessons, and grades. One is that a direct link can be drawn from lesson planning to taught lessons and ultimately to grades achieved. The other is that grades are the ultimate measure of success for a student and a school.

Unfortunately, both assumptions are oversimplistic and dangerous. There are many factors which determine grades that are not accounted for by a lesson observation or planning sample. More worryingly, in the desire to improve grades, we forget they are a measure of value, not value itself. In chasing higher and higher grades many schools have harmed the shared values that should be the true measure of success. Values such as kindness, and love of learning.

One of my guilty pleasures is watching Antiques Roadshow. Ever since 1979 the BBC TV show has been giving expert appraisal to antiques brought in by members of the public. In 2011, Ed Balls, former Chancellor of the Exchequer, was quoted as saying

> I cry at the Antiques Roadshow, you know, when someone comes in with some family heirloom and it's often the last bit in the programme and the expert says: 'Do you know how much this is worth? It's valued at X thousand pounds'. And they say, 'I'm amazed it's worth that much, but it means more to me than money.' Incredibly emotional.[2]

Value is hard to define. It is intangible and elusive. Because it is hard to articulate, value is often inferred through alternative or 'proxy' measures (often numerical). In the Antiques Roadshow, the expert judges the value of an antique in terms of money, but this is just a proxy. For the owner, money cannot measure value.

Numerical Proxies are used to represent value in all kinds of fields, and they often serve a useful purpose. However, they can also have unexpected and perverse consequences (see Tables 1.2).

In all the examples shown in Table 1.2, numerical proxies for value are widely used to allow comparison and judgements of success and failure to be made. Numerical proxies are useful for focusing people's attention and efforts on particular important areas of concern. However, proxies only represent value, they are not valuable in themselves. A good set of exam results should not be impressive in itself, but because it represents a student who is bright, hardworking, resilient, and positive. These are the values we aspire to and when this is forgotten it creates the kinds of negative issues shown in the final column of Table 1.2. In education, no numerical proxy alone can measure value.

Winning is everything?

A useful comparison can be made with the world of sport. This is one area where the measurement of results really does matter. Fans are attracted by the spectacle of the crowds and feats of skill or beauty. They see value in fair play or emotional connections with the team, but ultimately, it is results that matter most.

In August 2016, Liverpool played Burnley in the Premier League and lost 2-0 despite enjoying 81% of the possession. This broke the record for a team dominating possession but still losing. There would have been very few Burnley fans that day complaining about the lack of quality of their side and few Liverpool fans would have felt much consolation in having been the 'better' team. The score is an appropriate numerical proxy for the value of a team. Winning is important, and rightly so.

But is education like sport? In education, we are now used to the idea that the value of a school can be captured by a variety of proxy measures. Currently, it is 'Progress 8', but before that it was levels of progress and before that 5 A*–C. Just as in the movie charts or football league, schools are ranked according to their performance in these numerical proxies and judged to be outstanding, good, or worse accordingly. This system has been the reality for schools for so long that it seems to be common sense – part of a natural order that we see reflected in sport, and business. We lose sight of the fact that using proxies to rank schools is part of a 'marketisation' process which is manufactured. It is artificial, partial, and inappropriate.

Marketisation side-lines the promotion of values in education in favour of a narrow focus on proxy measures and the actions that inflate them. Mechanistic lesson observations and data analysis become all-consuming rather than a proxy for something much more important but harder to measure. Schools are faced by a choice between running their school according to strongly held values and sacrificing more or fewer of these values in favour of maximising numerical proxies. Numerical proxies which can be ranked and used as evidence of success or failure in a pernicious system which uses the veneer of data to mimic objectivity.

Table 1.2 Values and proxy measures

Field of endeavour	Exemplar values	Proxy measures	Strengths of proxy	Issues caused by proxy
Health Care	Respect and dignity Quality of care Compassion Working together	Waiting times Length of stay Number of patients treated	Numerical measure allows comparison Encourages efficiency (shorter waiting times)	Neglect of non-targeted activities Distortion of priorities
Sport	Ambition Inspiration Social connection Fairness	Ranking of performance	Numerical measure allows comparison Clear measure of success Inspires competition and improvement	Financial mismanagement Cheating Drug abuse
Social Media	Freedom of speech Open access to large audience Increased competition and innovation	Number of followers/likes/retweets	Numerical measure allows comparison Individuals able to build large audiences and attract sponsorship/advertising	Mental health issues amongst users 'Race to the bottom' in content attracts followers Successful independents taken over by a few social media giants
Education	Social justice Empowerment Fairness Inspiration	Progress 8/Attainment 8/Disadvantaged Pupils	Numerical measure allows comparison Encourages efficiency (improved outcomes)	Neglect of non-targeted activities Distortion of priorities 'Gaming the system' Stress and mental health issues

What lies beneath?

On the surface, all may seem well; attainment goes up. However, too strong a focus on results alone distorts actions and leads to perverse compromises of values. In sport, athletes take performance-enhancing drugs to gain marginal advantages, in business, companies cut corners for short-term gain, and in education schools pile more pressure on staff and students leading to increases in anxiety and stress. Like the top 10% of the iceberg, all we see are the gleaming successes, whilst under the waterline and out of sight, problems lurk.

In his memoir, 'People Like Us', Hashi Mohamed writes that the intense focus on teachers and schools in recent years "may have led to more people passing more exams, breaking the link between poor attainment and class or wealth ..." (what we see) "... but it has piled pressure on to teachers and students, making the experience of education profoundly stressful and unrewarding"[3] (what we do not see). Repeated surveys show high proportions of teachers feeling so undervalued that they want to quit the profession[4] and according to the TES, one-third of teachers leave the profession within five years of qualifying.[5] Meanwhile levels of youth mental disorders are at record levels.[6] On the surface things look good, but underneath, marketisation has created a culture with such an unrelenting focus on numerical proxies that the values they are supposed to represent (e.g. inspiration and empowerment) are being destroyed. The price is being paid by our young people and school staff now, but it will be paid by the whole of society in the future.

The future of values

When Ofsted criticises schools for 'gaming' the system and 'failing to act with integrity',[7] it is hard to accept they are not doing so with their tongue firmly in their cheeks. It is the accountability system, for which they are responsible, which encourages activities such as 'off-rolling' and qualification tourism. The latest inspection framework may be seeking to address some of these issues, but local school ecosystems are well established. 'High-performing' schools live off their reputations and attract the most ambitious and capable families whilst other schools do their best with the remainder. The resulting fossilisation of school reputations leads to well-rehearsed negative consequences: prohibitive property prices in the catchment areas of 'in-demand' schools and perpetuation of the social status quo. Without concerted effort change will not come.

There are signs that things may be starting to change. In their latest inspection framework, Ofsted seems to show an increased sensitivity to the importance of values (the brackets and bolding are mine):

> "Inspectors will **not use** schools' internal assessment data as evidence"...
> **(what we see)** "The following activities will provide inspectors with

> evidence ... discussions with curriculum and subject leaders and classroom teachers ... observations of and interviews with pupils"... **(what we don't see)** "Leaders have a clear and ambitious vision for providing high-quality, inclusive education and training to all. This is realised through strong, shared **values**, policies and practice."[8]

It is encouraging to see these references to values from Ofsted. There is an opportunity for teachers to seize this opportunity and be bold in advocating for the return of values to the heart of education. But what should these values be?

> All the big debates in education are about format. About delivery ... Education is consistently presented as a means of adaptation – as a lubricant to help you glide more effortlessly through life ... The focus is on competencies, not values ... On "problem-solving ability," but not which problems need solving.[9]

We have lived so long within this system that even talking about values seems naïve.

The case for optimism

The debate about the future of education has already begun. In a press release from June 2019 the CBI gave us the following headline: "Education System Leaving Young People Unprepared for the World of Work.[10] Another headline reads, "Robots will destroy our jobs – and we're not ready for it".[11] It is often quoted that a large proportion of the jobs available to our youngsters in the future have yet to be invented. Where does this leave education? Should we be anticipating the skills our students will need in twenty years and designing a curriculum with values fit for that future?

Pessimists might say that we are facing a dystopian future in which rapid developments in mechanisation and artificial intelligence will cause major dislocation. Labour markets will be revolutionised with automation making huge numbers of routine, low-skilled jobs redundant. At the same time, a highly skilled elite will earn massive returns from inventing and adapting technologies to fill more and more of the niches previously reserved for the masses. This dystopian future will see a social apartheid between the haves and have nots. Gated communities will spring up in which the ultra-rich live lives beyond the dreams of avarice whilst the unwashed masses roil outside the gates.

The response of education in this scenario could be to play a desperate catch-up game. We must prepare as many of our students as possible for the technological whirlwind. This view contends that education needs to provide the skills that technology requires. Schools should compete in an arms race trying to keep up

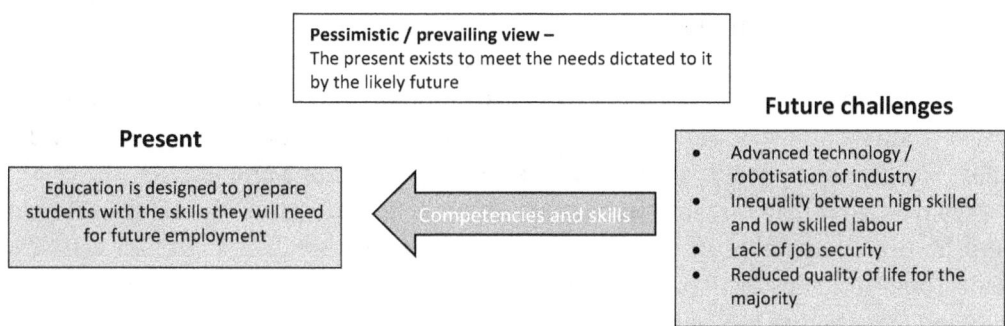

Figure 1.1 Pessimistic future view

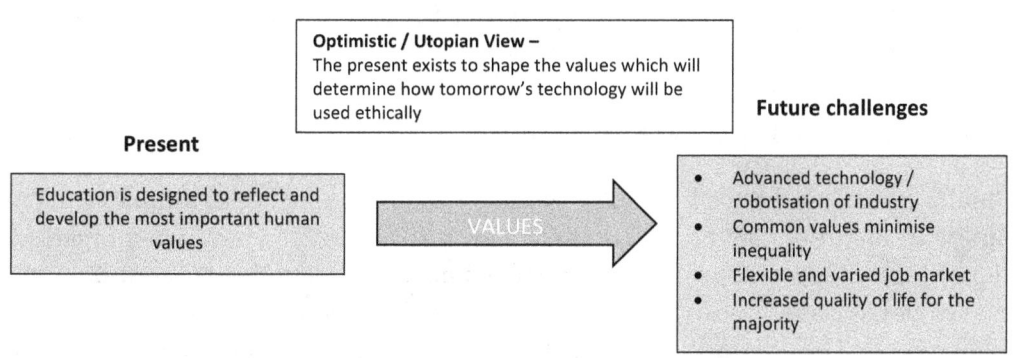

Figure 1.2 Optimistic future view

with changing technologies as they evolve and destroy existing jobs and communities (Figure 1.1).

Fortunately, there is an alternative, more optimistic, view which says that none of this is inevitable. The way that society, and the economy, develops is not predetermined. It comes about through the actions of millions of individuals who are guided by their personal values, and hundreds of thousands of groups who are guided by their shared values. Rather than merely responding to the needs of a seemingly organically evolving economy, education has a critical role to play in deciding the speed, route, and destination of economic and technological travel. There will be huge pressure to surrender to a logic that places skills above all else, but educators need to be confident in asserting the importance of values (Figure 1.2).

Shaping the future

The question for schools should not be what skills we **need** our young people to have in the future but what skills do we **want** our young people to have in order to shape the future. Then, instead of anticipating and adapting, we'd be focusing on steering and creating. Let us make sure that students can study foreign languages, drama, music, PE, and a full range of subjects for as long as possible. We want the best scientists and economists in the world coming out of our schools, but we want them to appreciate beauty and fairness as well as equations and graphs.

We need to reflect on what we want in the future. More time for leisure, friends, and family? Being able to enjoy a vibrant and diverse environment? Maximising individual incomes or maximising value for all? For too long we have had an education system that has been forced to sit on the side-lines when it comes to conversations about value. In the prevailing system, value in the economy has become synonymous with price, and value in education has become synonymous with exam results, regardless of what lies underneath. This book is intended to play its part in changing the prevailing system and reclaiming values as the ultimate purpose of education.

The score will take care of itself

Finally for this chapter, a legendary sport coach once published a volume of memoirs with the title "The Score Takes Care of Itself".[12] In his view, when organisations share values and goals, team members make the right decisions at the right times, and success follows. Focusing on values in education is not only right, it is also good. The argument is not that values are more important than results but that focusing more on values will relieve the pressure associated with succeeding at all costs. Establishing shared values is a good way to help schools succeed more often. If the right values are used to set the agenda in schools, results will 'take care of themselves' to the benefit of staff, students, and the communities they serve (Tilting the table 1.4).

Tilting the table 1.4 The future of values

Complete the table below on your own or with colleagues:	
What do you want for the future of your young people?	How can you work as part of a team to help this future become a reality?

Conclusions

- All teachers should be involved in agreeing shared values.
- If personal values conflict with shared values, it causes anxiety due to 'cognitive dissonance'.
- Shared values enable a complex organisation to function with unified purpose.
- Value is elusive so is often inferred from numerical proxies, for example, examination/test data which are generated by actions.
- Focussing on numerical proxies alone can destroy the values they are supposed to represent.
- Education should play a part in setting values for the future, not simply respond to values set elsewhere in the economy/society.
- Focussing on values is not just right, it is good.

References

1. Forster, E.M., 1927. *Aspects of the novel*. Penguin Classics.
2. https://www.theguardian.com/politics/2011/nov/21/ed-balls-cry-antique-roadshow.
3. Mohamed, H., 2020. *People like us*. Profile Books.
4. https://www.theguardian.com/uk-news/2021/apr/08/one-in-three-uk-teachers-plan-to-quit-says-national-education-union-survey
5. https://www.tes.com/news/recruitment-third-teachers-leaving-profession-within-5-years
6. https://www.bbc.co.uk/newsround/54644470
7. https://www.standard.co.uk/news/education/schools-gaming-exam-system-at-the-expense-of-poorer-pupils-says-ofsted-a4340001.html
8. Ofsted School Inspection Handbook – 2019.
9. Bregman, R., 2017. *Utopia for realists*. Bloomsbury.
10. https://www.cbi.org.uk/media-centre/articles/education-system-leaving-young-people-unprepared-for-modern-world/
11. https://www.theguardian.com/technology/2017/jan/11/robots-jobs-employees-artificial-intelligence
12. Walsh, B., 2009. *The score takes care of itself: My philosophy of leadership*. Portfolio.

2 Tilting models

It proposes Internalising the doughnut model to achieve success that is sustainable and kinder to students and staff. Finally, it proposes a method for formally adopting the doughnut model into development planning.

One of the joys of teaching is that no two days are the same. Hot weather makes the pupils lethargic whilst wind makes them wild. Optimism abounds at the start of term but exhaustion reigns by the end. Inspections, parental concerns, budget pressures, and human nature can combine to make schools bewilderingly dynamic.

In this chapter we will consider how symbols and models can help us to tame this complexity. We will look at the underlying assumptions of models and how the goals they focus on shape the actions of students and staff. We will think about how models help to construct goals and how these goals can either reinforce the shared values of the school or override and obscure those values. Finally, a new model of school development will be introduced which aims to strike a balance between retaining a strong resemblance to the real world whilst simplifying reality enough to be useful (Tilting the table 2.1).

What is a school?

Schools are enigmatic. Their essence does not reside in any one element, such as uniform, behaviour policy, or intake, but in the interaction of all the functions and stakeholders of a school and how they change over time. Sometimes, seemingly minor changes can lead to major effects in the way a school is perceived. Perhaps a change in behaviour policy or uniform is considered so fundamental as to threaten the values and identity of the school. At other times major upheavals, such as a new building, leave the perceived identity of a school untouched, if its values are strong and remain intact.

Schools are 'imagined realities'. Organisations of people and resources which are perceived to be a coherent entity. Businesses, sports clubs, and political parties are other examples. To thrive, they depend upon a common perception of the values they represent. This perception must be widely shared and consistently

Tilting the table 2.1 Thought experiment

Consider the following scenarios and discuss whether each would change the school enough for it to be considered a completely new school:
- the uniform changes
- the name changes
- the SLT are removed and replaced by external candidates
- the site is sold and a new school is built nearby
- the intake changes to become more/less selective

promoted in the stories that people tell each other about the organisation. 'As long as this communal belief persists, the imagined reality exerts force in the world'.[13]

In this chapter we will look at how an effective, shared model can reinforce values and inform the stories that are told about our schools. We will consider the dangers of models which over-simplify reality and create a focus on goals which overshadow and obscure values. We will also introduce a model that helps to maintain shared values, even when these values are translated into concrete goals and come under daily pressure within complicated and dynamic schools.

The power of a picture

One of the earliest known examples of written communication is a voucher for beer. It is a small lump of baked clay, about the same size and shape as a computer mouse. The voucher is currently housed in the British Museum, and was made in Southern Iraq almost 5000 years ago. It dates from a time before money, when workers received rations of beer as part payment for their labour. The symbols etched into its surface represent jars, bowls, and people. Before the development of phonetic letters, bureaucrats in Mesopotamia, Egypt, China, and Central America were instead using symbols to record important information – receipts, bills, and inventories.[14]

Symbols are simple pictures that represent a more complicated reality. In the ancient world, they were crucial for organising and controlling people gathering in rapidly swelling cities. Today, they retain their usefulness in an increasingly fast-paced and complex world which sometimes leaves us short of the time or mental capacity to absorb and comprehend written messages (Table 2.2).

What makes a good symbol?

Effective symbols are bold, simple, and reminiscent in some way of the reality they are representing. This could be an important or urgent need (toilet symbols, road signs), or a complicated idea which is difficult to summarise in written language (a pleasant place for a picnic). Symbols become imprinted in our minds and can be recognised almost instantaneously before we are consciously aware of their presence.

Tilting the table 2.2 The power of symbols

Do you know the meaning of the following symbols?

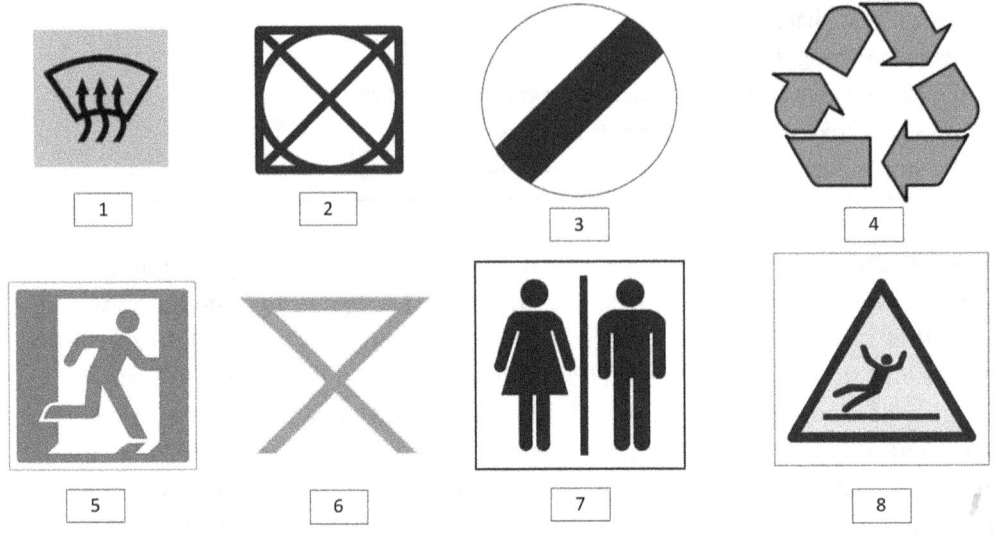

This is good news for us if we are seeking to escape from a burning building and good news too for advertisers if they want to sell us fast food on a busy city street.

As well as helping us when a need is urgent or important, more complex symbols are crucial for helping us to conceptualise difficult or abstract ideas. These more sophisticated symbols are called models and help us to capture ideas and structures which would be difficult or impossible for a human mind to comprehend without help. Maps are one example. A map is the simplification of a landscape designed to help us navigate, plan, and communicate with others about the real world. Whenever an entity grows in complexity to the stage where no one person can understand it fully, a model is required.

Schools require a model. Not only do they consist of concrete elements, such as buildings, equipment, teachers, pupils, and resources but also abstract ideas such as teaching, learning, respect, kindness, and aspiration. No one person can fully comprehend the operation of every part of the system or the interrelationships between these parts. For this reason, models are necessary to help us understand and organise schools.

'The Curve' – the world's most influential symbol

'The Curve' is arguably the most influential model of the twentieth century. It illustrates the ideal path of GDP over time (GDP stands for 'Gross Domestic Product' and is a measure of the wealth of a country). Growth in wealth builds a collective sense of well-being, but losses spark anxiety amongst politicians, economists, and

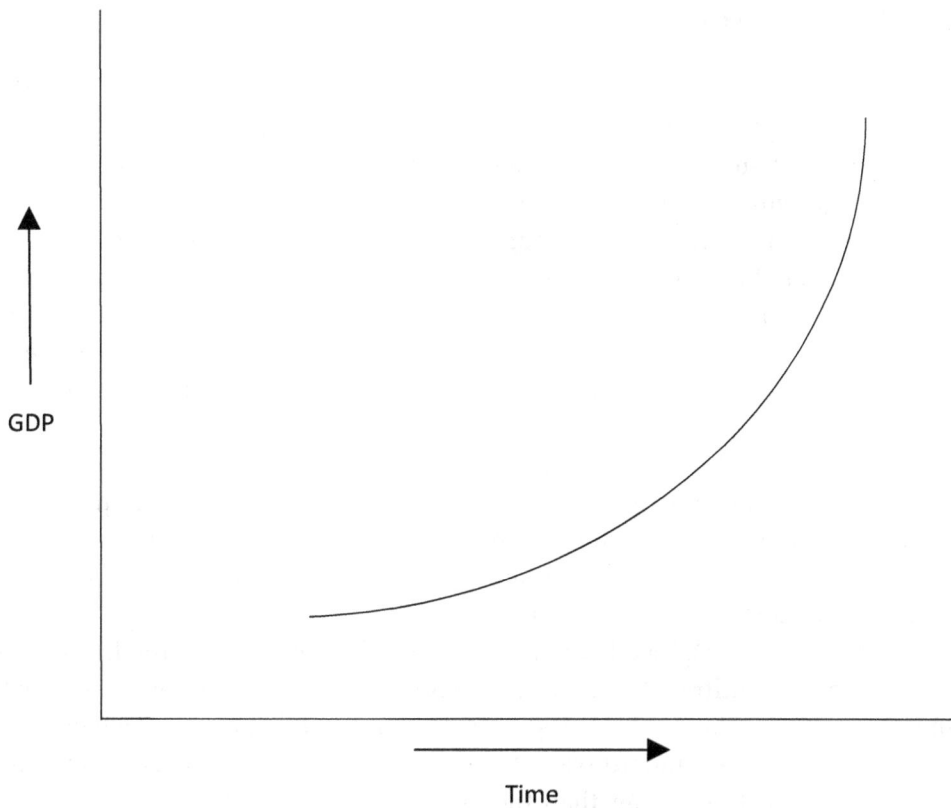

Figure 2.1 The curve symbol

the public alike. The curve shows an ideal of wealth increasing uninterrupted into the future at an ever-increasing pace. To conform to the curve, politicians chase economic growth as a primary aim of economic policy.

Despite its widespread acceptance and familiarity, the measure of GDP was only formulated in the United States as recently as 1934. This was a time of national emergency in the United States, as the economy went through the great depression. President Roosevelt wanted a single measure of how much stuff the economy was producing so he could judge the effectiveness of his policies for recovery and GDP was the answer. Prior to this, the size of economies was estimated using numerous measurement systems for thousands of products and services, each with their own idiosyncrasies.

The simplicity of a single measure for the whole economy was beguiling for journalists and politicians alike. One, simple measure made it easy for politicians to celebrate success and journalists to hold power to account. The use of GDP quickly spread across the world, as did the widespread and uncritical acceptance that growth is desirable. The graph of GDP increase which I will call 'the curve' shown in Figure 2.1 became a symbol of prosperity and success. A bold and simple image, rather than a graph, which embodied the values of optimism and success that have fired western economies ever since.

What lies beneath?

In many ways growth is good. The curve is very useful for comparisons, planning, and holding people to account, but it also creates serious issues. The existence of this dominant image, and the focus it places on simple measurements and continuous growth, discourages value judgements and obscures undesirable outcomes. The assumption is that all economic growth is good. But are sales of cigarettes as valuable to society as sales of gym memberships? Does the expansion of the gambling or arms industry represent the same value for society as expanding green technology or healthy food? The curve makes no distinction. What we see is economic growth; social and environmental harm lie beneath, undetected, or ignored.

The other issue with the curve symbol is that it presupposes that wealth can grow for ever. It is this desire for continuous and never-ending growth that can be argued to have led directly to the current environmental and climate emergencies. The race for ever greater levels of wealth being has led to habitat destruction and a warming climate.

All of this would be of academic interest only if it were not for the fact that the curve symbol has infiltrated thinking in a whole variety of other fields. Proxies for value, as we saw in Chapter 1, are seductively simple, and applying the logic of the curve has become the standard way of demonstrating success across society. Each year's number must be higher than the last, regardless of whether this is visitor numbers at museums, patients treated in hospitals, or progress 8 scores. Questions about whether constant improvement is sustainable, or desirable are side-lined, obscuring any harms or unintended consequences that lie beneath.

The dangers of unintended consequences

In the early 1900s the French colonial government of Vietnam came up with a brilliantly simple plan to reduce the numbers of rats that were plaguing the capital city, Hanoi. Locals were offered one cent for every rat they could prove they had killed. To claim the bounty, it was necessary to produce the proof of death: a rat's tail. This seemed a brilliantly simple way to reduce rat numbers and tens of thousands of tails were duly handed over. Yet the problem did not seem to be getting any better.

It was only after several months that the ruling powers began to smell a rat (sorry) when an increasing number of sightings of tailless rats were reported. Instead of killing healthy rats, people were catching them, chopping off their tails, and releasing them to produce more and more baby rats, with tails. Add to this the sudden boom in the trade for rats from the surrounding countryside, and even the growth of a rat farming industry, and the catastrophic, unintended consequence of the policy was revealed. The bounty was cancelled, and people had to learn to live with rats.

Unintended consequences in education

In 1992 the UK government placed a high priority on improving the English school system. A National Curriculum had been introduced in 1989 and testing followed in 1991. The next stage of its plan was to introduce school league tables which ranked schools according to the attainment of their pupils at the end of Year 11. Ranking schools by this simple measure in league tables would facilitate greater parental choice and encourage improvement through competition, part of the marketisation process discussed in Chapter 1.

It seemed like a simple solution. One measure is easy for schools, parents, and inspectors to understand and year-on-year improvement of this simple measure would represent success. Schools were incentivised by high-stakes inspections to take the new system seriously. This was the logic of the curve.

Unfortunately for the government, schools responded like the rat-catchers of Hanoi. They were asked to prove their success by one simple measure, so they concentrated disproportionate time and energy on fulfilling that measure. Despite the measure being designed as a proxy for success, because of the high stakes involved, the measure itself became success in many schools. They were incentivised to concentrate on borderline pupils around key grade boundaries at the expense of others. Some narrowed their curriculum to 'teach to the test', entered students multiple times, and for qualifications that were perceived as 'easier'. The increasing pressure on schools to achieve in high-stakes tests is widely acknowledged to have contributed to increasing rates of dangerous stress for staff and students. Like the French in Vietnam, the government got what it asked for but not what it wanted or needed.

By the time the government realised the problems it had created, many of the negative unintended consequences of competition had become entrenched in the school system. Attrition rates in the early years of teaching remain worryingly high and mental well-being amongst our young people is more fragile than ever before. Yet, the mindset of judging the value of a school by a narrow set of statistical criteria still prevails. The stakes are still high and perverse incentives will continue to skew the priorities of school leaders as they are placed under ever more extreme pressure for constant improvement by the logic of the curve. Regardless of the hidden costs, if they are rewarded for tails instead of rats, schools will continue to play the game, and nothing will change.

Simple problems

All problems cause stress and yet there are some problems that people love to face. Many people subscribe to a particular paper because of the challenge provided by the blend of problems contained in the puzzle pages. Taking on the challenge of a Sudoku puzzle or Crossword can be distracting and fulfilling, although occasionally frustrating. The reason we enjoy these problems is that they are predictable.

There are rules and fixed parameters. We know that there is a solution, and we know when we have found it. There are a variety of learnable strategies which will lead to success often enough for us to remain interested, but not frequently enough to become bored. No matter how complicated the puzzle, they remain simple problems.

Too often we treat the challenges we face in schools as simple problems. We limit the variables, make assumptions, quantify, and rank issues for simplicity. We create definitive and knowable success criteria and apply the curve model of success: ever-increasing growth. The models we create in this way are very useful. They help to clarify the goals we are working towards in a precise way that allows us to judge whether these goals have been achieved. Using such models allows us to promote accountability by judging the success of ourselves and others against seemingly concrete measures.

Problems arise however when we forget that these are mere models: simplifications of the real world. However sophisticated the model, it only represents the real world. The philosopher Alfred Korzybski encapsulated this idea in the phrase "the map is not the territory".[15] In other words, a model derived from something should not be mistaken for the thing itself. However comforting the feeling of control derived from capturing the essence of a school in a model or data set might be, this kind of complacency can lead to disastrous unintended consequences (Tilting the table 2.3).

Tilting the table 2.3 The map is not the territory

Discuss what you think the message of this cartoon might be.

In the cartoon, the walker has utter faith in their map. They forget that the map is a model of reality but not reality itself. Despite evidence to the contrary (wet feet), they continue their journey in the belief that, if reality differs from the model, reality must be wrong.

Problems caused by simple models

Examples of problems caused by overestimating the reliability of models but underestimating the complexity of a system and can be seen in many fields as well as schools. Models are used widely to predict and explain the way that systems work. For example, the world of finance pays huge sums to experts who develop exact models of the operation of money markets. Algorithms that predict movements of share or commodity prices control the movements of billions of dollars every day by the second. Such models can seem to have tamed complexity and eliminated risk. However, the uncritical acceptance of simple models can have unintended consequences that prove catastrophic.

In the 1990s, a company called Long Term Capital Management (LTCM) built a business whose model was built on an algorithm which appeared to have eliminated risk from trading. By assuming that prices at the large scale behaved predictably, despite small-scale variation, LTCM felt able to assure investors that their money was safe. Returns of 20%, 43%, and 41% in its first years of trading seemed to back up the claims. However, when the Russian economy collapsed in 1998 the company lost half a billion dollars in one day and went bust.[16] Ten years later, the global recession of 2008 was again triggered by banks being seduced by what their models told them should happen and ignoring the evidence of what really was happening around them.

Models and schools

Comparing reality to a model as a guide is fine, but we need to be wary of elevating the model to the level of infallibility. Simple symbols and models have a place in the physical sciences where all variables can be predicted and controlled, but in the real world of finance, or schools, more complex but 'fuzzy' models better represent the many variables faced by leaders at all levels. A fuzzy model doesn't pretend to be exact, but includes ranges of success, measured in different ways, that are more reflective of the world's complexity.

Life is messy. The real world rarely presents us with simple problems that have neat, knowable, and predictable solutions. In schools, there are usually several possible outcomes for any decision we take. Our job is trying to choose the best (or least bad) of alternative likely outcomes. Schools experience many problems simultaneously which overlap and interact. They involve people who are difficult to predict and impossible to fully manage. We rarely possess all the information we think we need to take a decision and find it impossible to fully model the likely consequences of those decisions once taken. We do not need models that claim to replicate the real world exactly, we need fuzzy models that resemble the complexities of the real world enough to be useful as a guide, but not so precisely to be trusted as a map.

The case for complexity

Isiah Berlin did more than most to raise interest in the idea of complexity or 'value pluralism'.[17] He recognised that in the search for a just society it is necessary to pursue a multiplicity of goals which are not necessarily consistent or compatible. In the same way, for a school to flourish it must pursue a variety of goals which may not only be contradictory but are also likely to be 'incommensurate'. This means that there is no common standard of measurement by which to compare them. How can you compare a school's achievement in the areas of anti-bullying and extracurricular participation or academic progress with student resilience or well-being?

In schools, the incommensurability of competing goals has led to the dominance of goals which are quantifiable (exam grades, attendance figures), above those which are less easily measured (joy of learning, personal fulfilment, mental health). In the process, strongly held values are lost in favour of goals which are measurable.

The myth that the main goal of education should be ever-increasing performance in a small number of measurable goals needs to be challenged. The logic represented by the curve symbol, adopted from economics, represents an alluringly simple image but it belongs in a laboratory where all variables can be controlled. We need a model of schools that embraces the complexity and unpredictability of school life and gives wriggle room for life's uncertainties.

Such a model needs to give equal weighting to both quantifiable and qualitative goals. It must accept that decisions made to impact on one area of school life may have unforeseen negative consequences on another area which may not be quantifiable. If we are to expose the harms which have previously lain beneath the surface, we need a model that is authentic enough to reflect the dynamic and unpredictable realities of school life (Table 2.4).

The doughnut school model[18]

In her book 'Doughnut Economics', Kate Raworth proposes a more nuanced model to challenge the symbol of the curve. It seeks to acknowledge the importance of multiple, incommensurate measures of success and keep them in balance without automatically preferencing any one of them. We can learn valuable lessons from Raworth's work.[19]

The model she uses to illustrate her idea is shaped like a ring doughnut. It has an empty core within which basic social functions and needs are not being met. On the outside of the doughnut social needs are met but at the cost of increasing environmental damage. Between these two areas, which represent the doughnut itself, lies a safe space within which the needs of humans are balanced with the needs of the environment.

Tilting the table 2.4 Incommensurate and conflicting goals

Apart from published performance measures, what should be the five most important goals of your school?

1.

2.

3.

4.

5.

Compare your list with someone else if possible.
Which of these goals can be quantified?
Which of these goals are likely to come into conflict with each other? How?

The ring doughnut is underpinned by the 'Goldilocks' principle. Within the core is an area which is 'too cold', outside the ring conditions are 'too hot' and within the ring is 'just right'. It is this element of her model which we can adapt for schools, as shown in Figure 2.2.

The doughnut school model

The 'Manic School'

In some schools, performance measures may be high, but this will be to the detriment of the mental health and well-being of staff and students. This kind of manic school may be characterised by multiple initiatives, conflicting goals and unrealistically ambitious targets and time frames. Consequently, attendance and mental health issues become a problem. Low morale, burnout and, paradoxically, reduced performance follow on. Manic schools are 'too hot' even though they may be achieving highly on a superficial level.

The 'Mired School'

These are schools which fail due to complacency and doing too little. Perhaps they are surviving on ill-informed word of mouth and slick marketing which no longer reflect the truth. It may be that good relationships between staff and students obscure a lack of aspiration hidden beneath the harmonious surface. For whatever

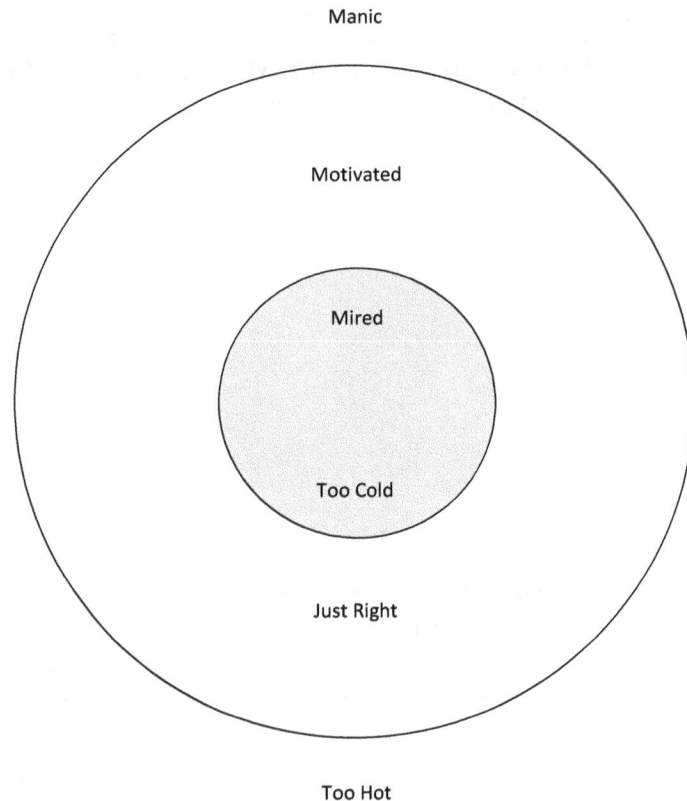

Figure 2.2 The doughnut school model

reason, a school that is mired, or 'too cold', leaves potential unfulfilled and aspirations unmet. These schools are metaphorically 'stuck in the mud'.

The 'Motivated School'

In contrast, a motivated school consists of staff and students who are strongly challenged, but carefully supported in achieving their goals. Characterised by high levels of discretionary effort from staff and students, built on shared values that are in harmony with goals, staff feel valued and able to be open in critiquing and suggesting improvements to systems and strategies. Students are aware of how to self-regulate their studies and where to get support when they need it. Such schools will achieve consistently well in performance measures but also have high levels of staff and student confidence and satisfaction. This is the ideal.

The dangers of binary measures

Standard development and appraisal models set a specific, measurable target for each desirable goal. However, one specific and measurable target limits outcomes to two 'binary' possibilities, success or failure. If the result fails to meet the target it is a failure, if it exceeds target it can also be construed as a failure (to set a sufficiently challenging target). Either way, failure is the most likely outcome. For this reason, specific and measurable targets can easily damage morale and stifle motivation.

One of the strengths of using the Doughnut Model is the avoidance of this kind of high stakes, binary judgement. Instead of a success target for each goal we have a success range. Provided the result lies within the 'just right' category it is neither too cold nor too hot and therefore a success. The encouragement this provides sustains a motivated school.

Dividing the doughnut

The other main strength of the doughnut model is its ability to show all the most important goals of a school on the same diagram despite their incommensurability. The fact that all the goals sit side by side as slices of the doughnut gives each value and draws out the potential conflicts and unintended consequences that may exist between them. Figure 2.3 shows a divided doughnut for which I have selected exemplar goals (Tilting the table 2.5).

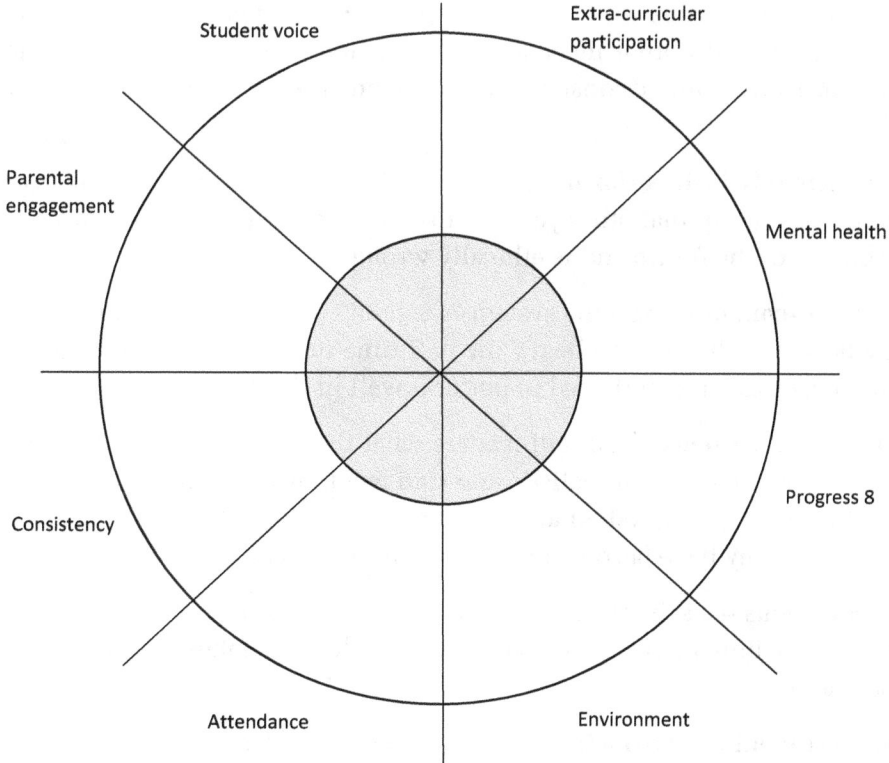

Figure 2.3 Dividing the doughnut

Tilting the table 2.5 Setting goals

Decide on your eight top goals for this academic year, draw your own diagram and label each slice of your doughnut.

Ceilings and floors

The doughnut model does not deny the need to assess performance and hold professionals to account. Rather it is a means to hold the school to account over a broader range of more appropriate judgements. To be effective each goal needs to have defined floors below which performance is judged as being too cold and ceilings above which it is too hot. In this way accountability is maintained but spread across a wider range of areas which are more reflective of the true values of a school.

It is generally easier to define the floors than the ceilings. We are used to, and find it more instinctive, to define the level below which we would be worried about poor performance rather than the level above which we would start to worry about unintended consequences. Specifying some levels of success as being 'too hot' is the unique part of the doughnut approach, and initially more difficult to arrive at. The key here is to imagine at what point seeking to increase performance in one area would lead to negative consequences in a different area. There are several different mechanisms by which overperformance in one area could cause unintended consequences and push another area out of the 'just right' zone:

1. **Unsustainably high performance** – a school is concentrating so many resources on one year group that other year groups are being neglected. This is storing up problems for the future and is ethically wrong.

2. **Staff over-commitment** – the systems a school is employing to address an issue may be successful but too heavy on staff time or energy to be justifiable. Staff need to be fresh and enthused to perform well in the classroom.

3. **'Fudging' of systems** – staff tell leaders what they want to hear rather than the truth. If your goals are unrealistic and staff feel they are unachievable, they may resort to playing the system and covering up issues that will raise their heads later when they have become more difficult to address.

4. **Narrow focus** – a school is too focussed on one goal and becomes determined to meet an unrealistic target which is 'too hot', it takes its eye of the ball elsewhere.

5. **Parent/student dissatisfaction** – a school has pushed so hard to achieve a goal they have lost the support of students and parents. Think carefully about coordinated, communication with home that is two-way and responsive to concerns.

6. **Duplication of work** – a school has allocated plenty of staff to a goal, but they are uncoordinated and duplicating some roles whilst others remain unfilled.

7. **Student over-commitment** – students have so many opportunities to participate in extracurricular activities, revision sessions, and other out of hours support, that the most conscientious are stressed. Make sure you monitor participation carefully.

8. **Increasing mental health issues** – so many demands are being made on students that their mental well-being is negatively impacted (Table 2.6).

Figure 2.4 shows the earlier doughnut model with added ceilings and floors. I include this for comparison. It is not intended as definitive. Every time a group of staff collectively construct a doughnut model for their school, the discussion is as important as the finished product. These discussions will energise collective thought and consolidate values. Every doughnut should involve unique goals, ceilings, and floors reflective of the specific values and challenges of its school.

The power of the doughnut

When we begin any new activity as novices everything feels challenging. New drivers crunch the gears and find parking highly stressful. New teachers construct detailed lesson plans which can initially construct and make them awkward in front of a class. Learning to use the doughnut model is similar. It represents such a change in mindset that at first it may feel tricky to implement. One of the strengths of the doughnut model however is the memorability of the image and the questions it represents. At its most simple, the doughnut symbol will prompt you, and others, to ask whether your school is manic, mired or motivated and reflect on how things could be done differently to the benefit of students and staff.

Over time, driving becomes second nature and teachers internalise the disciplines that formal lesson planning is designed to develop. As you become more confident, you may want to adapt the doughnut into the detailed planning of your school's development (see Table 2.1) but perhaps the biggest impact will be the internalisation by all stakeholders of the doughnut model itself. Images are powerful

Tilting the table 2.6 Setting success ranges

For each goal you chose in Tilting the Table 2.5, decide the signs of being 'too cold', 'too hot' and 'just right' – some may be quantitative and some qualitative
TIP – a sign that something is in the 'too hot' section might be that it is likely to push something else out of the 'just right' section – remember that your resources (time, money, staff) are limited.

Table 2.1 Doughnut development planning

Goal	Specific targets			Strategies	Staff	Check points
	Mired	Motivated	Manic			
1 Increase proportion of students engaged in extracurricular activities	<50% of students engaged and student voice poor	50%–80% of students engaged and student/staff voice good	<80% of students engaged but student and/or staff voice poor	Involve student council in promotion Student ambassadors Part of reward system Payment of staff Termly audit and survey of staff/student voice	IPF	Dec. March June
2 Provide good support for students with mental health needs	Systems not in place/coordinated/insufficient for demand	System in place and coping with stable number of referrals Positive student voice	High and increasing referrals – systems struggle to cope – duplication of work – staff burnout	Review current systems for referral Change duty rotas to free time for counselling Provide mental welfare training for whole staff Staffing review – numbers and skills	UDK	Sep. Nov. Feb. April June
3 Maximise positive attendance	Attendance <95% Lack of consequences – parent voice unsupportive	Attendance 95%–98% Clear systems operating smoothly Student and parent voice supportive	>98% Student welfare/health affected Dubious systems in operation Parents unsupportive	Assemblies regularly highlight the benefits of attendance Regular review of systems and staffing Parental information campaign Student voice and involve student council	ITA	Sep. Nov. Feb. April June

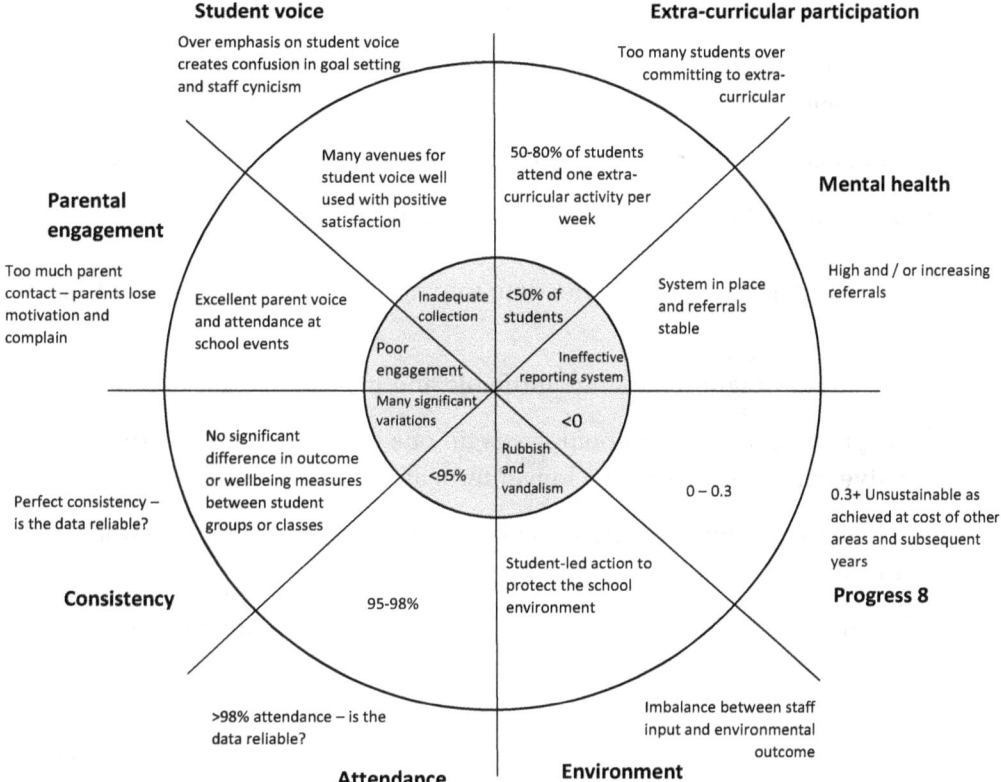

Figure 2.4 Ceilings and floors

and the doughnut is a bold and memorable symbol that will quickly infiltrate the shared consciousness of your school and bind staff and students together. It will underpin and nurture the shared values and stories that maintain your school's 'imagined reality'.

Schools that are driven by the right values and guided by the right model will set complimentary goals that enable challenging targets, which reinforce shared values, to be met. Using the doughnut model will bring success that is kind to students and staff as well as sustainable in the long run.

Conclusions

- Models help us to understand complex schools.
- Models help to translate shared values into concrete goals.
- Oversimplified models obscure the values they are supposed to represent in favour of achieving goals.
- The curve symbol has infiltrated thinking in education and is dangerous because it:

- encourages focus on too small a range of goals,
- creates the illusion that improvement can carry on for ever without negative consequences,
- obscures negative consequences that lie beneath superficial success.

■ The 'Doughnut School Model' corrects 'curve thinking' by:

- defining a zone of success rather than relying on binary judgements of success or failure,
- giving equal weighting to unquantifiable and measurable goals,
- raising awareness that over-emphasis on one goal in the short term can have negative consequences in the longer term and for other goals.

■ Internalising the doughnut model will lead to success that is sustainable and kinder to students and staff.

■ The doughnut model can be formally adopted into development planning.

References

13 Harari, Y.N., 2011. *Sapiens*. Vintage.
14 MacGregor, N., 2010. *A history of the world in 100 objects*. BBC Books.
15 Korzybski, A., 1931. *A non-Aristotelian system and its necessity for Rigour in mathematics and physics*.
16 Smith, E., 2012. *Luck*. Bloomsbury.
17 Berlin, I., 1969.
18 Clemmet,J.,https://www.tes.com/magazine/archived/why-school-improvement-doughnut.
19 Raworth, K., 2017. *Doughnut economics*. Random House.

3 Tilting evidence

The chapter proposes that, for this reason, 'SMART' targets should be 'SMART-IE' targets – indicative and expendable. This would reduce the incentive to manipulate evidence and increase the honesty of discussion. Next, the chapter proposes that the more complex a role is, the more difficult it is to assess success – the 'inverse skills problem'. Another issue is the difficulty of judging the significance of evidence, and whether one event causes, or merely coincides with, another. Finally, it considers the many traps that we can easily fall into when interpreting evidence which lead to bad decisions and bad policies.

The film 'Paddington 2' is that rare thing, a sequel that many view as being better than the original. Loved by children and adults alike, since its release in 2017 it has made over 200 million dollars at the box office and won numerous awards. However, when reports hit the media in the summer of 2021 that it had replaced Citizen Kane as the best film of all time, eyebrows were raised.[20] It attained this accolade when a negative review of Orson Welle's classic from the 1940s was discovered. Until that point Citizen Kane had 100% positive reviews and was tied first with Paddington 2, according to a film review website. It made a great story and aggravated film buffs for a day or two, before fading from the headlines.

This is a relatively trivial story; however, it illustrates a need that seems to be central to human identity. We love to compare, quantify and rank things. It is tempting to imagine cavemen sitting round a fire and discussing their best stone tools. In our own time, this need to quantify and rank phenomenon is reflected in the number of websites dedicated to top ten lists and the online review culture that produces star ratings for everything from holiday cottages to propelling pencils.

The doughnut model, introduced in Chapter 2, encourages us to balance the needs of multiple goals. By doing so, we can maintain the breadth of focus which reinforces shared values. Multiple goals require multiple types of evidence both qualitative and quantitative and yet educational data tends to be heavily skewed toward the numerical. This chapter will consider the strengths and weaknesses of quantified evidence, seek out potential pitfalls and think about how to avoid them.

It will review the types of evidence used to compare and rank schools and reflect on the evidence schools collect, why we collect it and how it is collected. We will consider how evidence collection itself can sometimes change the phenomenon we are seeking to capture. Finally, we will review how much trust we place in our evidence, the errors we make in interpretation, and how to avoid them. Most people would recognise that judging the best film ever, solely using numerical data, is just a bit of fun. Unfortunately, in schools, the same processes can be taken much more seriously with profound consequences for students and staff.

Maths anxiety

Recent times have seen significant, positive increases in people's awareness of the damage done by ignorant attitudes towards race and sexuality, for example. However, one area of life about which it still seems socially acceptable to remain ignorant is quantification. To cover up personal anxieties about our grasp of maths, it seems ok, even for highly skilled professionals, to sometimes profess ignorance and abdicate responsibility for mathematical analysis. This is a kind of learned helplessness and manifests as a lack of confidence or will to question quantitative evidence. Such attitudes elevate numerical evidence above its natural position as a useful tool for analysis to a mystifying and infallible measure of truth.

There is a danger that quantitative evidence can attain a pseudo-magical status. Those initiated into its secrets are left with disproportionate power over those to whom its operation remains a mystery. Open debate can be stifled when appeal is made to mathematical evidence which seems objective and incontrovertible but in reality is neither. Quantification can obfuscate as well as illuminate.

Quantitative data is a necessary and incredibly powerful tool for improvement when it is used appropriately and proportionately. Quantification can help us to know if we are achieving our goals and upholding our values; whilst ignorance of maths blurs outcomes and erodes our ability to take good decisions. For this reason, a positive approach to the use of numerical evidence is needed. Numbers are used widely to support all kinds of theories, and the acceptance of learned helplessness towards quantitative evidence leaves schools vulnerable. Vulnerable to exaggerated claims for the strength of numerical evidence, which lead to bad decisions and poor outcomes for students and staff (Table 3.1).

The strengths and limits of quantitative information

The viewing figures for 2020 are very useful. An industry demands them, and a complex process exists to produce them. TV viewing figures determine the price that TV companies can charge for advertising slots. Without them, the advertising industry would waste money producing adverts that few people would see. In addition, for academics, viewing figures can be useful for spotting social changes revealed by our changing viewing habits. However, viewing figures alone do not

Tilting the table 3.1 Top 10 TV programmes of 2020 (UK)[21]

Programme and date	Audience (one decimal place)
Prime Ministerial Statement 10/05	18.9 million
BBC News Special 23/03	14.6 million
I'm a Celebrity – Final	14.4 million
An Address by Her Majesty the Queen 05/04	14.3 million
Strictly Come Dancing – Final	12.6 million
Des (Drama)	11.9 million
The Great British Bake Off – Final	11.8 million
The Salisbury Poisonings (Drama)	11.7 million
Britain's Got Talent (Final)	11.4 million
Ant & Dec's Saturday Night Takeaway	10.8 million

What does the ranking tell us about TV watching habits in 2020?
Which of these programmes do you think was best?
TIP – for training, muddle the list up and ask participants to guess the order.

reveal all. Advertisers also want information about how content is watched, who is watching and how this translates into increased sales.

Viewing figures cannot tell us which programmes are 'best'. This is a subjective judgement. The programmes were produced for different audiences and had distinctive goals. To gauge their quality, we would need to collect feedback information from the viewers and experts. However, feedback is not as easy to collect or analyse as viewing figures. It costs time and money to find people and interview them, so we often judge the success of programmes on viewing figures alone. This can lead to programme-makers focusing on making shows that are above all popular, and neglecting considerations of taste, accuracy, and bias.

As for the TV industry, at least part of the attraction of quantitative evidence for schools lies in its relative ease of collection and presentation. Finding out what people think takes time and yields results which are difficult to interpret and understand. Numbers seem concrete and reliable. They are relatively easy to generate and, for a society that shrinks away from maths, ideal for 'proving' an argument. However, as with TV, over-reliance on numerical measures can lead to schools focussing on what generates good numbers, rather what generates good education.

Synthetic quantification

Synthetic materials are those which are made to imitate a natural product, for example, synthetic sweeteners. Made to imitate sugar, they provide the sweetness, without the extra calories or tooth decay. Synthetic sweeteners have many uses in the fight for better health; however, they are not perfect. An initial hit of sweetness often leaves behind a 'synthetic' aftertaste. Over time, regular users stop noticing, but synthetic products are never the same as the product they imitate.

I use the term 'synthetic quantification' to describe numerical measures that are formulated to measure characteristics in the social, rather than the physical, sciences. This includes statistics to measure important elements of education. Synthetic quantification is used to capture progress or achievement and it does an invaluable job. It allows us to compare performance and decide on plans of action. However, it should always leave a synthetic taste in the mouth. When we stop noticing that they are synthetic, we can mistake the numbers themselves for actual progress or achievement and this is where the problems start.

Lord Kelvin was an eminent mathematician and physicist in the Victorian age. For him, "when you cannot express it in numbers, your knowledge is of a meagre and unsatisfactory kind". However, education is not physics. The aim of physics is to establish a unified set of laws that govern matter, motion, and energy. For this endeavour, quantified evidence is the only means of testing relationships and validating hypotheses. However, for social sciences, such as education, quantification is different. It is a tool for taming a world in which there are no unifying laws. Although very useful, it sits alongside other, equally important, but neglected sources of evidence.

In physics, numerical evidence represents carefully calibrated and unchanging scales with which to measure a predictable world. They remain unchanging over time and space. In contrast, social scientists synthesise numerical measures to collect and process quantitative evidence for a particular purpose. If a different expert were constructing the measure (or the same one on a different day) they may make different choices and generate different results.

Synthesised quantification helps us to understand an unpredictable world of human interactions. Problems arise in education however, when we confuse the synthesised quantification of social science for the universal quantification of physics. Quantitative data in physics, if properly obtained through experimentation, is objective, knowable, repeatable, and testable. In contrast, although synthesised quantification appears to allow objective comparison; because it is based on subjective information, it remains subjective despite any veneer of objectivity. This can easily be forgotten, with dangerous potential consequences, when such information is presented to a meeting on an impressive-looking spreadsheet or graph.

Quantitative revolutions

Studying education is a social science and using quantitative evidence in the social sciences is a relatively new occurrence. Subjects, such as geography, economics, and political science, all underwent quantitative revolutions in the second half of the twentieth century. Early work in these areas concentrated on describing their area of study, however, once the descriptive phases were complete, many social sciences were left with nothing new to say and without any underlying theory to explain or predict. Increasing computer technology in the 1960s and 1970s allowed geographers, economists, and political scientists to revitalise their subjects by seeking universal mathematical laws that explained relationships and could be applied and tested using formula and models.

By the 1980s and 1990s many felt that the focus on mathematical modelling had gone too far. The human element was being obscured by a spurious scientific veneer. New social scientists became increasingly interested in topics revolving around race and gender conflict about which mathematical analysis had little to say, and the paradigm shifted again. Today, these subjects attempt to balance scientific approaches of data collection and hypothesis testing with an appreciation of the human dimension and all the unpredictabilities that this entails.

The education quantitative revolution

Since the introduction of national testing and league tables, educational analysis has undergone its own quantitative revolution. The aim was to escape a dominant descriptive environment in which public information about schools was largely conveyed through word of mouth and reputation. More objectivity was required.

The gap between image and reality could be vast and to close this gap, the government sought to collect quantitative data which could be used to test perceptions of schools and help parents to make informed decisions. As a result, we are no longer short of quantitative information about schools, and much of this information is incredibly useful (Tilting the table 3.2).

The paradox of data is that we need large amounts of varied data to accurately reflect the complex nature of school environments, but this can easily cause confusion. Focussing on smaller data sets enables clarity but can be oversimplified to the point that it starts to obscure or distort reality. Accountability has had many benefits in improving educational standards; however, there are dangers both in collecting too much and too little data. We can be in such a hurry to quantify our educational experiences that there is a risk of losing the human dimension.

Tilting the table 3.2 What evidence "have school's collected and continue to collect?"

Four are listed below – try and think of at least six more

- Progress 8
- Grade 5 and above in English and Maths
-
-
-

- Attainment 8
- Attendance %
-
-
-

Note: Each of these may be further analysed according to, change over time, pupil characteristics breakdown, subject breakdown, class breakdown.

Why we need good quantification in education

Teachers are experts in education. Society delegates the job of teaching to expert teachers in the same way that it delegates healthcare to nurses and doctors and car maintenance to mechanics. Because no individual can gain all the skills to remain happy, healthy, and safe in modern societies we delegate different roles to different experts for the benefit of all. It is the job of teachers to turn society's values into goals and actions in the classroom. However, this separation of consumers of education (students and parents) from providers of education (teachers) creates issues of quality control. If they do not understand what is happening in the classroom how can parents know if it is being done well?

I have the same problem when I take my car to the garage. When I am told a job is going to cost me a lot of money I have two choices; as someone with little knowledge of engines, I can take it to a different garage or I can trust the expert and pay for the job to be done. In the same way, when parents are unhappy with a school, they can either move their child to a different school, or they can trust the expert. This trust is built on professional training, years of experience, and strong relationships.

In small societies, where people know each other well personally, and by reputation, trust develops over many years and the system works well. However, in larger, modern societies where local knowledge is poor, the argument is that old-fashioned attitudes of deference towards experts lead to poor service and slipping standards. Deference reduces the scrutiny and legitimate challenge which keeps experts on their toes. For this reason, we need impartial evidence about hospitals, garages, schools, and everything else.

Hospitals have the CQC, garages have trading standards, and schools have Ofsted. Society delegates to them the job of interpreting the complex processes of healthcare, car maintenance or teaching and providing the evidence that makes them intelligible to laypeople. The ideal way to communicate judgements is quantification. Whether it is a five-star rating or an Ofsted rating, numbers are simple, concrete, and trustworthy. Numbers do not lie; or do they?

Who is collecting the data, and what for?

Schools consist of principals and agents. School leaders are 'principals' who rely on teachers as 'agents' to work on their behalf. The principals lead in establishing shared values and goals and are ultimately responsible for results. However, they rely on teachers as agents to carry out the work which yields those results.

In a straightforward workplace such as a factory with a simple manufacturing process, the principal would know their objectives and understand the processes needed to achieve these objectives. In a biscuit or sock factory, detailed instructions and daily production targets would be sufficient to ensure success. These could be issued to workers who would then be left to get on with the job with a greater or lesser degree of supervision.

Schools, however, are not straightforward workplaces. Objectives in schools may be poorly articulated or uncertain, problems dynamic, and the environment chaotic. In this situation, the principals cannot issue instructions to fit every eventuality and meaningful, daily, numerical targets are meaningless. They need teachers as agents who are experts in their field to set their own objectives and interpret and respond to complex situations minute by minute.

Despite the complexity of teaching and the expert standing of teachers, it would be naïve and irresponsible of the leadership in schools not to put some level of quality assurance in place. Numerical targets are set, and evidence is collected to check on progress towards these targets. Unlike the biscuit or sock factory, however, these measures and targets need to take account of the complexity of the process that is being assessed and the expert role of the teacher. Numerical evidence needs to be treated with circumspection and act as a stimulus for discussion rather than an objective, scientific finding.

Where there is a high degree of professional trust between leadership and teachers, targets and quantitative evidence can be motivational. Where more faith is put in the numbers than the professional opinion of the expert on the spot, quantitative evidence can be demoralising and misleading. It can also lead to a breakdown in the relationship between principal and agent that is counterproductive and damaging to both (Table 3.3).

Goodhart's law

I walked into my kitchen recently to find my youngest child shaking her phone rhythmically back and forth. I thought for a moment she was in a rage, but she informed me that she was 'completing her 12,000 steps'. When I challenged her that completing her steps in this way would not help her fitness, she assured me that she had done at least that number but that the phone had not recorded them. She gave further justification by telling me that some of her friends topped up their steps by taping their phones to a tumble dryer.

Achieving 12,000 steps, just like the story of the Russian nail factory, illustrates that when a measure becomes a target it often ceases to be a good measure as people will start to 'game' it. They change the way they behave in order to maximise the measure rather than improve the characteristic the measure is designed to represent. This phenomenon was first articulated by British economist Charles Goodhart and is known as Goodhart's Law.[22]

Producing one giant nail, or taping a phone to a tumble dryer, are examples of people responding perversely to imposed, quantified targets. Targets of this type encourage actors to game situations with perverse, unintended consequences (remember the rat-catchers of Hanoi). The act of trying to quantify an achievement distorts the achievement you are trying to quantify.

Tilting the table 3.3 Principal/agent problems

Read the following apocryphal story:

Stepan Pavlovich, greeted the factory foreman with a fixed smile. At last year's event, the two had clashed about the target for that year's production. Everyone seemed to think that Pavlovich had the power to choose, but the weight of nails for the factory to produce was decided in Moscow. Determined and confirmed by the flick of a pen belonging to a comrade whose signature could also sanction a one-way trip to Siberia.

To Stepan's surprise, the foreman flashed a toothy grin and thrust a meaty hand out in greeting. The two held an uncomfortable pose whilst photos were taken, and they took their chairs on the makeshift stage.

The foreman turned to Stepan, and whispered, "I think you will enjoy this year's demonstration Comrade Pavlovich. You know of my misgivings about the target, but my men have worked heroically and produced exactly the weight of nail asked for".

For the first time in three days Stepan felt himself relax. The foreman gave a signal, the factory doors slid open, and the band struck up a military march. A flatbed lorry slowly materialised out of the gloom of the interior. Cab freshly painted for the occasion and belching out smoke, it laboured under the weight of its cargo, hidden beneath a huge scarlet tarpaulin.

The lorry came to a halt in front of the stage, and to an accompanying fanfare the covering was pulled away. Stepan felt the colour drain from his face. Glinting in the weak winter sunshine was the most enormous nail. One, singular, perfectly formed but grotesquely large nail.

The foreman turned once more and held Stepan's gaze defiantly as he recited the exact dimensions and weight of the nail, before pausing and leaning in close. "I hear the sunsets in Siberia are spectacular at this time of year comrade".

Who was the principal and who was the agent?
What does this story illustrate about problems that rigid, quantified targets can cause between principals and agents?
How is this applicable to schools?

The reasons for numerical evidence are understandable. All schools are judged on their performance by a small number of numerical measures. The problem is that this top-down approach to evidence strains the principal/agent relationship and encourages Goodhart's Law to come into play. The leadership are ultimately responsible and need to supplement professional trust by checking the work of teachers. Most teachers understand that a degree of supervision is required, because of the importance and complexity of their job. They also realise that central collection of data can save time and render insights that were previously obscured. However, if targets are imposed with high stakes consequences or felt to be unreasonable, and if checks are disproportionate in terms of time and energy, they can result in a break down in the principal–agent relationship. Agents are tempted to 'game' the system with damaging consequences.

SMART-IE targets

'SMART' targets are well established in British schools as a way of ensuring accountability and driving improvement. Appraisal and school improvement targets are designed to be 'Specific, Measurable, Achievable, Realistic, and Time bound'. They are usually quantified and are useful as a target to aim for by which we can make judgements about success. Even with the best SMART targets, however, problems arise when they are imposed, unreasonable or come with high-stakes consequences.

If the consequences of meeting a target are extreme (pay progression, Ofsted judgement, etc.) there is a strong incentive for agents to game the system. At one end of the scale gaming strategies might include subtly manipulating data, being passively obstructive (deliberately missing meetings/deadlines, etc.) or intentionally obtuse. At the other end of the scale of seriousness are practices such as off-rolling, multiple exam entries, and massaging intake criteria.

SMART-IE targets are designed to address these problems. The 'I' stands for indicative and the 'E' stands for expendable. Targets should be treated as indicative because they are an indicator of something, but they are not a proof. If a target is not met it may be a significant sign, or it may not. The key part of the process is the discussion about why a target has not been met and what, if anything, should be done about it. Too often these constructive discussions do not happen because meetings become emotional. Too much weight is given to whether a rigid, numerical target is met or not. If a SMART target is missed people often either become defensive or deflated. Neither of these reactions is conducive to a productive discussion which reflects on past actions and makes plans for the future. For this reason, SMART targets should be indicative only.

SMART targets should also be expendable. It may be that as part of a discussion about whether a SMART target has been met it is decided to abandon or disregard the target. Perhaps it was the wrong target. Maybe you realise that if the target had been hit, it would have detrimentally affected one of the other goals in your doughnut school model. Perhaps you have learned something important whilst not hitting the target that will be hugely useful in another way. In any of those situations, why would you judge the process to be a failure? The target should be necessary, but expendable. SMART targets that are indicative and expendable (SMART-IE targets) lower the stakes, remove the incentive for gaming the system and enable a proper professional discussion about values and goals.

What evidence should we collect?

Our main intention in school should be to promote the shared values of the school community. However, we know that values are slippery and difficult to pin down. For this reason, we set multiple goals, each with its own success range within our doughnut school model. These success ranges should be expressed in SMART-IE

Tilting the table 3.4 What evidence should we collect?

In its report "Eliminating unnecessary workload associated with data management" (2016),[23] the Independent Teacher Workload Review Group came up with the following recommendations:

Be streamlined: eliminate duplication – 'collect once, use many times'

Be ruthless: only collect what is needed to support outcomes for children. The amount of data collected should be proportionate to its usefulness. Always ask why the data is needed.

Be prepared to stop activity: do not assume that collection or analysis must continue just because it always has.

Be aware of workload issues: consider not just how long it will take, but whether that time could be better spent on other tasks.

Discuss how your school's approach to data management measures up against these proposals.

Do any changes need to be made?

---

targets. But what evidence should we collect and how much of it do we need? (Tilting the table 3.4).

Millions of people watch The Grand National every year. Hundreds of millions of pounds are gambled, with many people who place a bet not gambling throughout the rest of the year. To experienced gamblers, it must be galling to see a once-a-year tipster, who decided on a horse simply because of its name or the jockey's colours, collecting their winnings. The veteran of the betting shops has carefully considered the previous form of the horse, how much extra weight it is carrying and how hard the ground is. Despite this extra information and no matter how experienced the gambler, the odds always favour the bookmaker.

Logic suggests that the more information we have, the more likely we are to make a good decision. However, whether we are deciding which horse to back, or whether our school is performing well, this does not always follow. Sometimes knowing more information just makes the decision more confusing. To avoid Goodhart's Law, schools should always ask themselves why they are collecting evidence and only collect evidence that will support outcomes for children, provided its benefit is proportionate to the time and effort required for its collection.

Difficulties interpreting evidence

Having collected evidence that is appropriate, proportionate, and balanced with workload, the next stage is interpreting what evidence can, and cannot, tell us about success in meeting the goals that underpin shared values.

Our brains are evolved to spot patterns and infer relationships between different events. This was crucial in keeping us safe when we lived in hunter gatherer groups many thousands of years ago. For example, if I ate a plant and then fell ill, I would not eat that plant again. If my illness was not caused by the plant but simply coincided with eating it, I may be missing out on an appetising treat, but the consequences are not fatal. However, in a modern age when there is so much more information available to us, and so many more potential relationships between events, this skill can cause problems. In a complex world it is unlikely that we will come across simple, direct cause and effect relationships between events. Yet our brains continue to tell us that such simple relationships must exist, and we find comfort in identifying them.

Dunbar's number, named after biologist Robin Dunbar, is the maximum number of people with whom it is thought possible to maintain a meaningful social relationship. Generally considered to be one hundred and fifty it is thought to be the size of the groups people lived in for hundreds of thousands of years prior to the advent of settled agriculture. Because our brains evolved in this setting, some believe that we find it hard to judge the accurate probability of events happening by chance. Small populations mean that many events, which we take for granted within settlements of tens of thousands, would be very rare in primitive tribes of one hundred and fifty. For this reason, we underestimate the possibility of specific things happening by chance and seek to infer causes and links between events. We tend to look for explanations to explain seemingly unusual events even when they may be entirely predictable and to be expected.

For example, the definition of a dormant volcano is one which has not erupted during a human lifetime. If people in ancient times, when life spans were short, had lived near a dormant volcano they could well have been unaware. Unaware of plate tectonics with no reliable way of passing experiences from one generation to the next and little friendly contact with other people, the first sign would be an eruption. In this situation, despite the volcano perhaps having erupted as little as fifty years before, they would over-estimate the rarity of the event and seek to explain it, often by supernatural means, perhaps throwing animals into the crater to appease the deities of the volcano. The same may have happened to people who were left-handed or babies born with cleft palates because these events may never have happened in a tribe of one hundred and fifty people but happen regularly in a city of one hundred and fifty thousand people.

Of course, this is just a theory, but as modern humans we remain experts at identifying patterns in evidence and speculating on causes. We have problems accepting that, in complex environments, sometimes things just happen, there is no simple explanation and therefore no simple remedy. Throwing someone into a volcano based on misconceptions about probability and causality is thankfully not an option. But the same errors of misinterpretation can lead to unfair and invalid judgements of cause and effect in schools with harmful consequences for students and staff.

Errors in interpretation

Lots of time and effort in schools goes into collecting and collating evidence, but often effective interpretation is neglected. Having gone to the trouble of collecting significant amounts of data it can be difficult to admit if it shows us very little of significance. There can be a pressure to act. The examples below are designed to illustrate different traps we may fall into when deciding what the evidence we have collected actually means (Table 3.5).

Hindsight bias

My family and I love watching 'Whodunnits' on TV together and speculating on who the guilty party is. An unstated rule exists that you must make your prediction before the killer is revealed on screen. The room of amateur sleuths will treat statements such as 'I knew it was him all along' with scorn if they have not already been made during the programme. Statements such as this illustrate a common mistake in interpretation known as 'hindsight bias'. This means revising the likelihood of an event happening after it has taken place or exaggerating how far we could have predicted it happening.

Our brains are superbly adapted to spot changes and patterns in complex data; however, if we infer causes for these patterns which don't exist, issues arise. It can be tempting to try and appear clever by retrofitting convincing explanations for events that have already happened for which there may be no causal relationship. Intelligent people spend time in meetings arguing for causes of events they would like to be correct rather than causes which are likely to be correct. If successful, and we are convinced of the wrong cause of an event, we may become overconfident about our ability to predict the outcomes of future events, 'if it worked last time, it will work again', with harmful consequences.

For example, imagine Mr Glumb was a demotivated teacher who had been told to attend an inspiring course on questioning by their line manager Miss Spark. Glumb seemed enthused by the course and, on their return, introduced a new technique he learned called 'Take5'. This involves every student having to count to five before answering a question. At the end of the term, results in all Mr Glumb's classes increased so dramatically that the head teacher, Mrs Staid, asked Miss Spark for an explanation. Eager to impress, Spark explained the inspiring course that she sent Glumb on and the Take5 strategy which had caused Mr Glumb's renaissance. The headteacher immediately saw that if it could work for Mr Glumb it would work for all teachers and decided to introduce Take5 across all subjects. Imagine Mrs Staid's disappointment when, having overcome considerable resistance and enforced a non-negotiable Take5 policy to all classrooms, results slumped across the school.

The headteacher had fallen victim to Miss Spark's hindsight bias. Mr Glumb's results went up but not because of Miss Spark or Take5 (which Glumb had ditched after a couple of weeks without telling anyone). The real causes of Glumb's success was that he had recently been given the all-clear over a health scare and whilst on the course had met and fallen in love with a colleague from the school down the road. His improved mood drove an increased sense of vocation and commitment which meant that he was planning and teaching better lessons and marking his

Tilting the table 3.5 What is wrong with that?

Each of the comments below illustrates one of several different mistakes in interpretation which are explained in the remainder of the chapter. Having read about each one, come back to the table and see if you can assign a specific error to each comment.

The errors are:

Hindsight bias, Attribution bias, Loss aversion, Volatility and time, and the Paradox of praise.

Comment	Interpretation error
"Twelve out of 18 subjects were below average, so we need a full-scale mock Ofsted to focus people's minds" (SLT member)	
"It wasn't pleasant being so tough on Miss P but her lessons have certainly improved" (SLT member)	
"Disadvantaged students did better for us than in other subjects so we must be doing something right!" (Head of subject)	
"Never mind that Chemistry did superbly, Biology and Physics were below average so I still think Science is a big problem (SLT member)	
"The boys were always going to do better in a single sex group for maths. I think it should be done for all subjects" (Head of English)	
"I'm disappointed. She was great last year and I told her so. This year it just wasn't as good. That's the last time I praise anyone for teaching a good lesson." (Line manager)	
"Geography progress in Year 8 hasn't changed since last month – they need a subject review" (SLT member)	
"The subjects who get the most investment get the best results. Without more money I can't improve things." (Head of underperforming subject)	
"We reduced PPA time and the results got better, we should have done it a long time ago" (SLT member)	
"Mr T taught a good lesson on Monday but on Thursday he was back to normal. I just don't think he's going to improve." (Head of subject)	

books more regularly. Misled by Miss Spark's hindsight bias, lessons in the rest of the school were slowed down so much by compulsory Take5 that teachers stopped asking questions completely and were instead planning lessons of silent reading.

Evidence prompts questions but does not provide proof. Be careful that explanations are not unduly influenced by what has already happened rather than what might have happened. There is no guarantee that just because something happens once, it will happen again in the same way, particularly if we identify the wrong causes of the event. If Miss Spark had noticed evidence of the upturn in Mr Glumb's results and asked him some questions, she would have found the secret to his success was not a new gimmick but likely to be planning and teaching good lessons and marking his books.

Attribution bias

One of the major issues which determined the 2010 UK general election was the global economic crisis. As Chancellor, and then Prime Minister, Gordon Brown had made a virtue of his prudence for over a decade and had even claimed to have eliminated boom and bust from British economics. As part of a New Labour government which was 'intensely relaxed about people getting filthy rich'[24] he had broken with Labour tradition and presided over light touch regulation of the financial system. Banking profits were booming and, with global deregulation of financial markets, the world's economies expanded and the UK economy experienced virtually continuous growth. Gordon Brown was happy to bask in the reflected glow of success.

This all changed once the global economic melt down took effect in 2008. The financial crisis had originated in the United States but had spread rapidly due to the lack of regulations in international finance. The very virtues that had allowed the UK economy to grow unchecked for more than a decade, now allowed the crisis to infect the UK financial system. Because of the lack of safeguards in the supervisory system he had overseen, and boasted of, the UK economy was in crisis. Brown justifiably claimed that the UK's financial worries were caused by issues beyond his control, but the voters did not believe him, and Labour was voted out of office.

This tale illustrates a very basic human instinct to attribute favourable events and results to our skill and unfavourable ones to bad luck or the incompetence of others. I think of it as football managers' bias as it is often exemplified during post-match interviews. After a victory they praise their team set-up, tactics, or excellent performances, but defeats are routinely blamed on poor refereeing decisions, bad luck, or unfair scheduling of matches.

In schools, attribution bias encourages us to overlook problems for which we might be responsible whilst claiming too much praise for issues over which we had little control. Imagine a secondary school who review progress data for students from different primary schools. They discover that one primary school's ex-students perform significantly worse than the others. If they attribute this lack of progress to the shortcomings of the staff or community of that primary school, whilst celebrating their own contribution to the progress of the high achieving students from other primaries, this is attribution bias. Over-estimating our contributions to successful outcomes and underestimating our role in failures leads to an over-developed sense of our own abilities. It also stops us taking responsibility for and learning from mistakes, stifling improvement, and failing our students.

Loss aversion

In general people hate to lose more than they love to win. To illustrate this, imagine that I offer you a 50:50 gamble based on the toss of a coin. If the coin lands tails side up, you lose £10. What would have to be the minimum amount gained, if the coin lands heads side up, for you to take the gamble? For most people it lies within the range of £15 to £25. This reflects the typical loss aversion ratio of between 1.5 and 2.5. Most people would need the chance of winning between £15 and £25 in order to risk losing £10.

Loss aversion has many interesting impacts on human behaviour. For example, professional golfers achieve more success with putts to save par than for birdie. Their preference for not losing a shot is greater than for gaining a shot, although both have the same effect on their final score.[25] Also, my cricket loving social media group buzzes with indignation when England lose a Test Match whilst victories rarely prompt more than the odd comment.

In schools this can have subtle effects which can be exacerbated by the widespread habit of rag-rating information. Red is chosen because it stands out much more than amber or green to highlight areas of concern. However, it can result in even relatively small differences in values on a spreadsheet or table attracting for more attention than the data justifies. The result is far more time and attention given to areas perceived as underperforming, which may be only marginally different (and perhaps with a reasonable explanation or within a margin of error) to areas which only receive cursory attention.

A useful question is to ask whether we have the balance right between rewarding 'strong' performance on the one hand and reacting to 'poor' performance on the other. Resentment and de-motivation is bred when we get this balance wrong.

Volatility and time

When the stakes are high, and we are anxious in any situation it can be tempting to shorten the time lapse between taking measurements. Checking your phone every minute for an important text or returning to the oven repeatedly to check on the progress of a cake are examples. However, checking evidence too often can cause 'boiling frog' syndrome. In summary, a frog dropped directly into a pan of boiling water will jump straight out. However, a frog dropped into a pan of cold water, which is then heated slowly, will not realise the danger until it is too late, resulting in frog soup. If we monitor any process in schools too often it can blind us to general trends. We only realise how much a situation has changed when it is too late to respond. Much better to space measurements so that we can observe significant changes that happen over weeks and months.

The other problem with short time frames is volatility. If you have just inherited a large sum of money and want to invest it in the stock market, you would be foolish to invest all your money in the shares which had increased in value most in the last twenty-four hours. Although you may get short-term gains over a day, they are likely to be wiped out by similarly rapid losses on the following day. Far better firstly to invest in shares which had shown moderate but predictable gains over a period of years or even decades, and then resist the urge to check their value on your mobile phone in real time, in favour of a regular check every couple of months.

In schools, short accountability time frames can create the illusion of failures, or successes, which are merely the kind of random fluctuations which we should expect in a complex system like a school. For example, if we check behaviour daily and find a sudden jump, this can lead to knee-jerk policy changes, particularly if this coincides with a senior leadership team meeting or governor visit. Ill-considered reactions to short-term fluctuations can be disruptive and ineffective, or even damaging to the long-run health of the school. Better to monitor less regularly and identify long-term trends rather than short-term 'noise'. This will yield far more appropriate and sustainable policy decisions.

The Paradox of praise

Hopefully, you can appreciate there is a mistake in the way the PE teacher interpreted their evidence (Table 3.6). They have failed to appreciate that in any progression of repeated activities, an extraordinary event is likely to be followed by a more normal one. Hence the ridicule preceded the improved performance but did not cause it. Likewise, after an exceptionally good vault, it is likely that the next attempt will be more ordinary, in other words worse. The praise did not cause poor performance, it merely preceded it. This phenomenon is known as 'regression to the mean'.

In schools, the paradox of praise may mistakenly lead to unsympathetic approaches being taken towards students, or staff, who are viewed as underperforming. It encourages a 'cruel to be kind' approach, which is not only extremely

Tilting the table 3.6 Is praise an effective motivator?

Read the experiment described below, carried out by a (thankfully) fictional PE teacher, and decide whether you think praise is a successful motivator.
Experiment to discover the best motivator for improvement in gymnastic performance
Method: After every vault I will give a high score and high praise to those that are good and a low score and ridicule to those that are bad. I will then record the score for the following vault of each gymnast to see whether praise or ridicule produces the biggest improvement.
Results
Following praise – only 18% of vaults achieved a higher score
Following ridicule – 76% of vaults achieved a higher score
Conclusion: My experiment clearly proves that the best way to motivate and cause increased performance in gymnastics is to ridicule the gymnasts. Paradoxically, praise causes poor performance

damaging and unprofessional but also morally wrong and ineffective. Where evidence suggests underperformance, students and staff need understanding, support, and encouragement to improve. Recommendations need to be clear and unambiguous but never unkind.

Avoiding errors

This chapter has introduced the idea of teachers being experts to whom society delegates the job of teaching our youngsters. Accountability demands that targets are set and evidence is collected to ensure that teachers receive appropriate levels of challenge and do a good job. However, we have seen that collecting evidence, when done badly, can be time consuming and even counterproductive, leading to perverse incentives to game the system. Once collected, evidence can be misunderstood and misinterpreted in ways that create skewed conclusions which lead to poor policies which harm students and staff (Tilting the table 3.7).

Perhaps the best way of collecting evidence is by respecting the role of teachers as experts in education. Structures that encourage teachers to reflect on and discuss their experiences and strategies with other teachers increase accountability and inspire professional growth. Carrying out small-scale studies which involve collecting evidence from their own classrooms, collaborating with others, and sharing their findings, reinforce the role of a teacher as an expert rather than merely an agent carrying out the instructions of others.

Tilting the table 3.7 Avoiding errors

Think about these strategies for avoiding interpretation errors. Reflect on how you could make sure these strategies inform your approach to data analysis.

Strategy	Explanation	Reflections
Allow for variability	Avoid binary thinking. Make room for a range of acceptable outcomes rather than high-stakes success or failure approaches.	
Do not mistake the absence of evidence for evidence of absence	Just because some of the most effective innovations cannot be quantified do not ignore them. The impact of sending flowers to poorly staff or writing personalised Christmas cards cannot be measured but that does not mean it is not significant.	
Judge by actions as well as results	Numerical evidence is only an indicator. Dig deeper before drawing conclusions. Professional dialogue, observations, work samples will provide a firmer foundation for judgements and a broader evidence base to formulate solutions.	
Embrace randomness	Try to approach data without preconceived ideas and do not ignore unexpected results. Perhaps you will discover novel solutions and innovations where you least expect them.	

Conclusions

- Education has gone through the same quantitative revolution as other social sciences with the same benefits and problems.

- Evidence is vital to help consumers of education (students and parents) understand the quality of the education they are experiencing.

- Quantitative evidence in education is useful but is 'synthetic' and should not be mistaken for the kind of objective evidence generated by experiments in physical sciences.

- When principals (leadership) impose targets and evidence collection on agents (teachers) it creates perverse incentives to game the system.

- SMART' targets should be 'SMART-IE' targets – indicative and expendable.

- The more complex a role is, the more difficult it is to assess success – the 'inverse skills problem'.
- We have difficulty judging the significance of evidence and whether one event causes, or merely coincides with, another.
- There are many traps that we can easily fall into when interpreting evidence which lead to bad policies and decisions.

References

20 https://www.abc.net.au/news/2021-05-02/paddington-2-citizen-kane-as-best-film-of-all-time/100109944
21 https://www.thinkbox.tv/research/nickable-charts/tv-viewing-and-audiences/2020-tv-viewing-report/
22 Elton, L., 2004. Goodhart's Law and performance indicators in higher education. *Evaluation & Research in Education*, 18(1–2), 120–128.
23 https://assets.publishing.service.gov.uk/government/uploads/system/uploads/attachment_data/file/511258/Eliminating-unnecessary-workload-associated-with-data-management.pdf
24 Mandelson – speech to executives in Silicon Valley, California, October 1999; Andrew Rawnsley Servants of the People (2000).
25 Kahneman, D., 2011. *Thinking, fast and slow.* Penguin.

4 Tilting teams

On 28 December 1978, a plane, United Airlines 173, took off from Denver, Colorado heading for Portland, Oregon. The flight passed routinely until, as the plane approached its destination, the highly experienced captain attempted to lower the landing gear. At this point, the crew heard a loud bang and the light to indicate that the wheels were safely down failed to light up.

The captain faced a dilemma. It was impossible to check the landing gear visually and the engineer could not confirm whether the wheels had lowered into place. Flight control advised that the wheels were probably down but there was no way of being sure. It was possible, but potentially dangerous, to land the plane without its wheels in place. What should the captain do?

He decided to wait. He put the plane into a holding pattern and circled the airport to give himself, and the crew, time to decide on a plan of action. This would have been a sensible move if the plane had plenty of fuel, but it did not. Fortunately, the engineer noticed that fuel was running low. Unfortunately, he did not share this information with anyone else. Despite it being a clear evening and being within sight of its intended destination, the fuel ran out, the plane crashed and twenty people, including the engineer, lost their lives.

The engineer on flight 173 was not afraid of the captain, he was not a terrorist, and he had no wish to commit suicide. The reason he did not alert the captain was because he did not wish to appear to undermine their status. Sharing the information could have implied that the captain had not noticed the fuel issue (which he had not) and might have been interpreted as criticism. Rather than infringe a social hierarchy, the engineer kept quiet, and twenty people died.

This chapter will investigate why teams of people malfunction. Why do members of a team, like the engineer, feel inhibited to speak freely, even when lives are at stake? Why do leaders of a team sometimes only want advice they like, regardless of its accuracy or helpfulness and why do members of a team conform to type over time, reducing diversity and narrowing opinions?

The pin factory

Without teamwork our society would be very different. It was teamwork that fired the industrial revolution by organising the armies of workers herded from Britain's fields and farms into the noise and dirt of its cities and towns. Adam Smith, commonly known as the father of economics, wrote about teamwork having observed operations in a local pin factory. Writing in 1776 he speculated that by breaking down the production of pins into at least eighteen separate processes, ten workers could produce, between them, 48,000 pins in a day. His estimate for the number that a worker on their own could produce was just twenty.

This process of breaking jobs down into separate tasks was termed the 'division of labour' and marked a break from the prevailing norm of craftsmen who were responsible for making a product from start to finish. The division of labour facilitates efficient working in three different ways: firstly, each worker becomes an expert in their role, enabling them to become highly efficient; secondly, the time which is commonly wasted whilst a worker changes from one task to another is eliminated; finally, specialist machines and processes are more likely to be invented which enable one person to do the work of many.

What Adam Smith observed in a pin factory two hundred and fifty years ago is still useful for analysing the work of teams in factories, and schools, today. The functioning of a school requires many different roles. Teaching, pastoral care, specialist support, curriculum planning, financial prudence, grounds maintenance, catering, and more. Although there is a 'headteacher' who is nominally responsible, these tasks are split into numerous different roles and responsibilities and divided amongst the staff. Just like Adam Smith's pin factory, the division of labour enables schools to run more efficiently by identifying and breaking down key jobs so that specialists can hone their skills and become experts (Tilting the table 4.1).

When people work as a pair, one person can manufacture whilst the other tests, and proportionally more aeroplanes are produced. The task could be made more complicated by introducing different elements to the process (e.g. add symbols to the planes, introduce different designs of paper aeroplane) but the principle remains the same. When we break a process down, and organise a team, each of whom specialises in a specific task, productivity increases (Figure 4.1).

There are many setting in which we could apply this idea. Perhaps A, B, C, and D are different stages of a factory production line or perhaps A is a singer in a band, B is plays lead guitar, C is the bassist, and D on drums in a pop group. In a school setting perhaps this is a senior leadership team with A being the head teacher, B being the pastoral deputy, C the academic deputy, and D the inclusion manager.

Teams that fail

The Generation Game was a BBC1 gameshow, originally presented by Bruce Forsyth, that ran on Saturday nights in the UK throughout the 1970s and 1980s. It involved

Tilting the table 4.1 Division of labour

Provide a group of people with a supply of A4 scrap paper and give them the following challenges:

A. Working on your own:

Make, and test fly, as many paper aeroplanes as you can in three minutes.

To be counted, all manufacturing <u>and</u> test flights must be completed within three minutes.

Each aeroplane must:

- Be made from one sheet of A4 paper only
- Look like a paper aeroplane (no scrunched up balls)
- Be able to fly at least three metres (each plane is only allowed one test flight)

Solo score:

B. Working in a pair:

Make, and test fly, as many paper aeroplanes as you can in three minutes.

To be counted, all manufacturing <u>and</u> test flights must be completed within three minutes.

Each aeroplane must:

- Be made from one sheet of A4 paper only
- Look like a paper aeroplane (no scrunched up balls)
- Be able to fly at least three metres (each plane is only allowed one test flight)

Pair score/2:

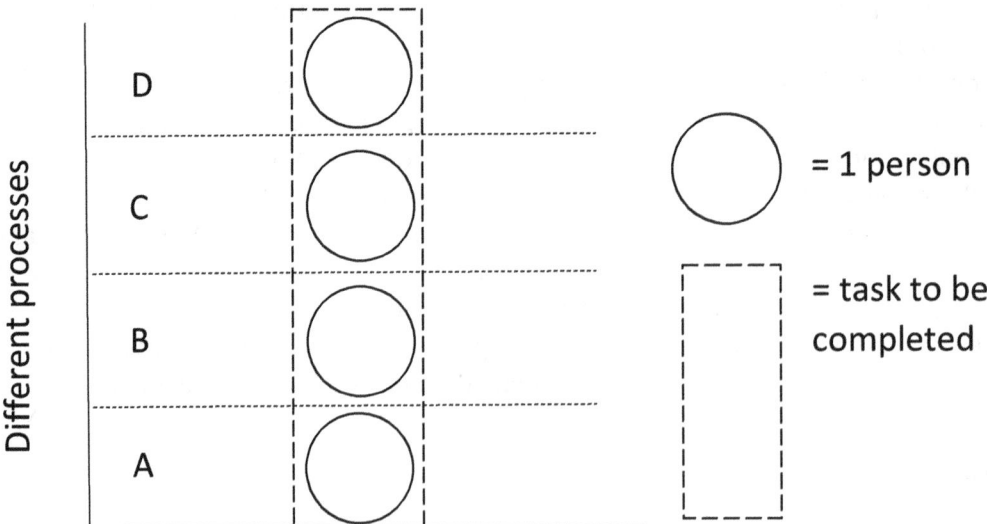

Figure 4.1 Division of labour

teams of two, from different generations of the same family, attempting to replicate a skill briefly demonstrated for them by a highly skilled professional. It could be dancing, pottery or cake decoration but the fun was in watching the team struggle to work together and produce anything that even vaguely resembled the intended product.

In a school, this type of team would not be entertaining. Lack of sufficient training and support may create a diverting spectacle for a TV show but would be disastrous in a staff team. School teams rely on shared values, but diverse skills and experience. No individual has the time, expertise, or experience to master all the roles which a school needs to operate smoothly. Providing clear roles, training, and support is vital to avoid the team failures that kept the nation entertained in the 1980s and 1990s. It is not surprising that unskilled, inexperienced, and poorly coordinated individuals struggle to make good teams.

Strange as it seems, however, skill, experience and coordination are not the biggest impediments to teamwork in schools. Training and mentoring can be provided to improve skill levels and bolster experience. Refinement of job descriptions, changing structures and more realistic expectations can help to improve poor teams made up of underperforming individuals. A far trickier problem is what to do when a team of high-performing individuals come together to make an underperforming team. Sometimes, teams can be highly experienced and accomplished with clearly defined roles and good team skills, but still fail.

Birds of a feather

In an age when sources of information are more diverse, paradoxically, thinking is becoming narrower. People choose their own social media, follow the feeds that reflect their own views and gravitate towards groups who think the same way. Therefore, greater polarisation occurs as people only voice their thoughts and emotions openly to friendly audiences. Validation is provided by like-minded souls and challenge is rare. Recent increases in extremism and political division are often traced back to this process.

The trait of choosing to mix predominantly with people who are like oneself is called 'homophily' and is a natural human trait. In an urbanised society where personal and familial relationships are weakened, we want to spend time with people like us. Unfortunately, however, if there is no diversity in our group, there is no one to challenge us when we are wrong. It is easy to feel so comfortable within your group that perspective blindness sets in. We are so used to our group's biases that we no longer see them. If we only ever work with people like us, we miss out on the kinds of diverse views which challenge dominant thinking and can stimulate novel solutions to issues.

Diverse thinking

Great teams, are united by values but also need diversity. In the heist movie, Oceans Eleven, for example, a team of experts is assembled by a leader who plans a daring robbery. Each of the team members has a different speciality: explosives, pickpocketing, electronics, disguise, etc. In addition, they are each from different ethnic, social, and economic backgrounds and of different ages (although they are all men). Ocean's skill is to unite this diverse team. Over the course of the film the team plan, clash, react, improvise, and ultimately succeed in their goal.

The differing demographic backgrounds of Ocean's eleven stimulate diverse thinking (cognitive diversity). The group coalesce around shared values (loosely defined as righting injustices and a shared love of living dangerously) but maintain fiercely independent ways of thinking. They evolve into a highly effective team with clear, independent roles who learn together under their leader's guidance and thrive. With all the necessary skills covered and diversity creating challenge and dynamism, shared values create the unity that leads to success.

Recruiting diversity

A firm that wants to broaden its diversity may engage a recruitment agency to head-hunt the best candidates. To avoid unconscious bias, recruitment tends to be 'meritocratic', based on technical skills and aptitudes but blind to colour or gender. For schools this is not always so easy.

Firstly, schools tend to operate on stable intakes of students and therefore budgets. It is therefore not usually possible to expand staffing by creating new posts, and recruitment happens only when people leave. Even if the school is aware of needing more diverse viewpoints, correcting this takes strategic planning over a prolonged period.

In addition, meritocratic recruitment cannot be relied on to create demographic or cognitive diversity due to 'knowledge clustering'. The candidates who score best in exams and tests are likely to be disproportionally drawn from high-performing universities and have attended high-performing schools. These candidates tend to benefit from high levels of social and cultural capital and be drawn from similar social and economic groups. Therefore, although demographic factors are ignored, the same types of people who went on the same types of holidays, attended the same schools and universities, and share a common culture are successful.

Although it is difficult to recruit diversity, it remains vital that schools continue to attempt to create a workforce that reflects the communities they serve as closely as possible. However, even demographically diverse teams do not necessarily create cognitively diverse teams. Homophily dictates that even diverse team members, who work closely together over long periods, often come to resemble each other.

Conversely, however, teams who lack demographic diversity can still possess dramatic cognitive diversity. The good news is that there are strategies you can use to develop cognitive diversity in your team even if it lacks demographic diversity. Teams that look the same can be encouraged to think differently, and to voice these thoughts, if proactive action is taken by leaders at all levels of school life.

The fab four

The success of the 2019 film 'Yesterday' provides an illustration of the enduring appeal of The Beatles. They are the best-selling music act of all time and a huge ongoing influence on popular culture. As well as their music, the personal and creative relationships between the members of the group also attracts attention. The Beatles were a team of white, working-class boys from the same northern city and provide a useful case study of how homogeneous teams can evolve, diversify and flourish.

Figure 4.2 illustrates the development of The Beatles' ways of thinking and skills over the band's lifetime. In 1963 the band were riding the wave of 'Beatlemania'. Pictures from the time show four young, white men with trademark 'mop-top' haircuts in matching stage suits. John Lennon and Paul McCartney wrote most of the songs together and they alternated on lead vocals. This period is illustrated on the left of Figure 4.2 with John and Paul overlapping in skills but all four of the band aligned in their thinking, as befits the most successful boy band in history.

In 1963 The Beatles were the masters of the three-minute pop song with their first three singles going to number one and sold-out concerts across the UK. Unlike other manufactured boy bands, however, The Beatles had two extraordinarily creative forces who were not content to continue churning out variations of the same output for their whole career. Throughout the rest of the 1960s, the group achieved the success and status that allowed them creative freedom from the demands of record executives.

By 1967, the band had given up touring and each member had broadened their musical skills and interests and taken time to pursue individual interests. This broadening of skills is shown by the growth of each member's circle in

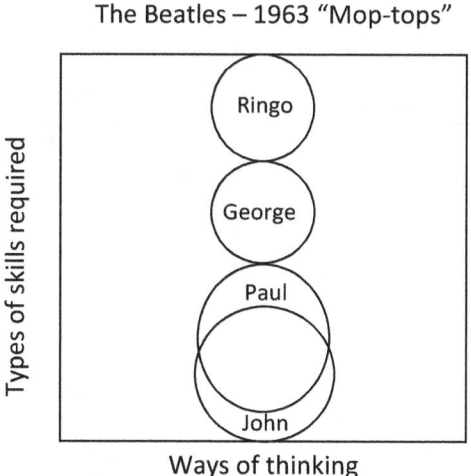
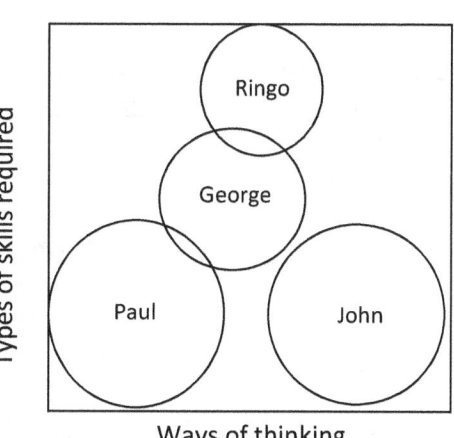

Figure 4.2 Team diversity

Figure 4.2 and the development of individual interests is shown by the movement of the circles from the vertical alignment on the left to the dispersion on the right.

The result was the release of arguably the most influential album of all time, Sgt. Pepper's Lonely Hearts Club Band.

Complexity and diversity

School teams operate in complex environments and need to be diverse if they are to succeed consistently. A cognitively diverse team with diverse skills will be successful because they are creative as well as functional.

TILT teams are the ideal. They combine highly diverse skills and experience with highly diverse ways of thinking. Although difficult to harness, when these teams coalesce around shared values, they provide the best example of the power of teamwork. When teams lack skills diversity, there will be gaps in the collective expertise that weaken the collective, creating groups of clones or an ill-disciplined rabble (shown in the lower half of Figure 4.3). If the team has diverse skills but familiarity has fostered homophily and led them to think alike, it creates a clone team, with less obvious, but just as serious, weaknesses as the individual clones or the rebellious rabble (Tilting the table 4.2).

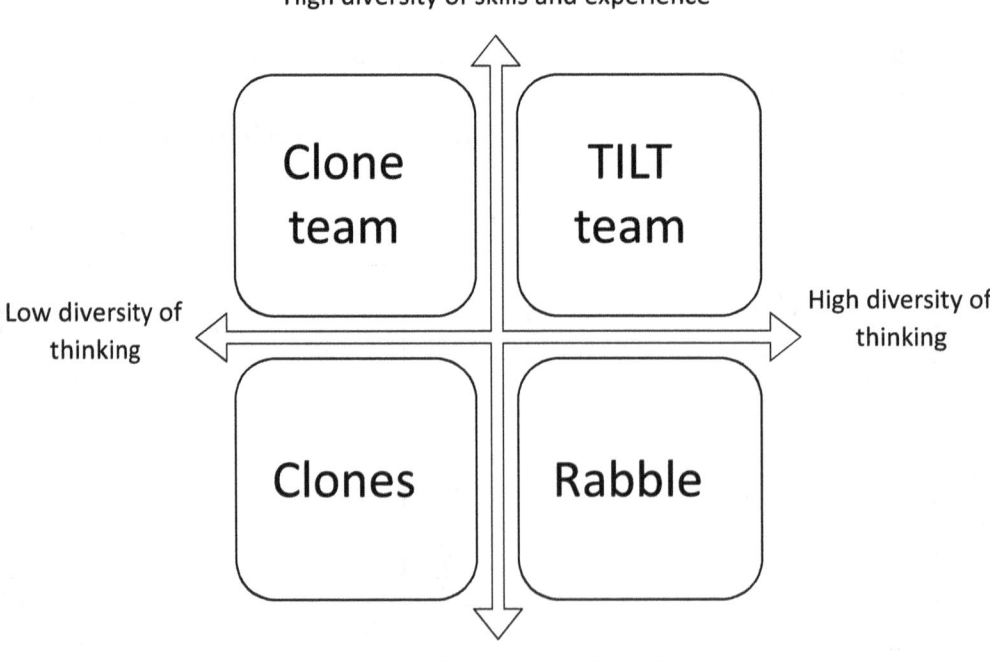

Figure 4.3 Team skills and thinking diversity

Tilting the table 4.2 Team diversity

The diagrams below represent a different team/group from Figure 4.3. Complete the table by highlighting the strengths and weaknesses of each.

Type	Characteristics		Strengths	Weaknesses
	Skills/experience diversity	Thinking diversity		
TILT team	High	High		
Rabble	Low	High		
Clones	Low	Low		
Clone team	High	Low		

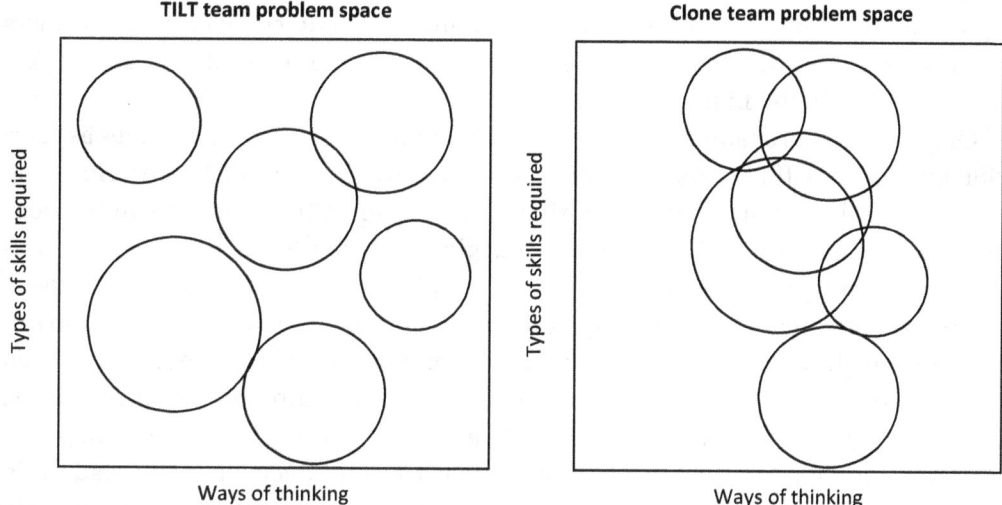

Figure 4.4 TILT team vs. clone team

Clone teams are worth spending a little more time on because they are the most difficult to identify. They have a wide skill set distributed across the team and seem well balanced. Meetings are harmonious and business is conducted efficiently. Clone teams are highly supportive of each other and good at explaining problems. They assess themselves as being successful and can provide evidence to support their claim. Clone teams are blind to their failings.

Figure 4.4 represents two teams working in a school. Each team consists of six members with differing levels of competence and experience (represented by the size of each circle). They might be a year team, subject, or senior leadership team and they face the same problem, represented by the problem space. The problem requires diverse skills and a variety of thinking skills to be solved optimally. Both teams possess the breadth of skills required but the TILT team cover a wider area of the problem space because of the variety of their approaches to thinking about the issue.

Clone teams tend to be happier and more certain of being right because members of the group provide validation more than challenge. The problem is often not that the clone team do not possess the ability to solve a problem, but that they fail to ask uncomfortable questions that expose the problem in the first place. Because they are not exposed to alternative perspectives such teams are more prone to being wrong but more certain of being right. Ignorance is bliss for a clone team.

Dominance versus prestige

Many mammal species live in highly ordered groups controlled by dominant individuals. Dominance in the animal kingdom is maintained through displays of aggression and strength to maintain control. In human teams, dominance hierarchies may develop inadvertently and be controlled in more subtle ways. The main sign of a dominance hierarchy in a team is undue deference given to the leaders of a team that can stifle debate. The story of flight 173 was caused by a dominance hierarchy within the flight team.

Only in extreme examples will dominance hierarchies assert themselves as coercion and intimidation or manipulation through reward and punishment. However, people in authority may have authoritarianism falsely attributed to them by those who lack confidence in themselves. Strategies designed to challenge hierarchies preserved through dominance are vital if cognitive diversity is not to be stunted.

Prestige hierarchies do not rely on dominance to be sustained. They are maintained through the development of authentic and enduring relationships between members of the team. These relationships are nurtured through social modelling and respect which lead to genuine sharing and cooperation. A culture of all group members giving and receiving honest feedback fosters deep dialogue leading to problems being identified and creative solutions applied. Cognitive diversity thrives in a prestige hierarchy (Tilting the table 4.3).

Tilting the table 4.3 Is dominance ever right?
Discussion point: Are there situations in which a dominance hierarchy may be the most appropriate structure for a team?

Scenario	Action. Dominant or Prestige?
Two proposed solutions to an issue have been debated during a meeting and no clear winner has emerged.	
The budget is tight, and savings need to be made.	
Ofsted have phoned to say there is an inspection imminent.	
A disclosure has been made about a member of staff.	
The school appraisal system needs updating.	
Insert your own	

Developing prestige

We have established that it is difficult for schools to increase demographic diversity through recruitment and even superficially diverse individuals can become aligned due to homophily. A dominant culture can suppress creativity, but simple and cheap strategies can foster a desirable prestige culture in which opinions and ideas are freely aired.

Team meetings, and how they are structured, provide a key opportunity to shape culture. For example, begin a meeting with a period of silent reading during which participants read a proposal that a member of the team has prepared in advance. If the identity of the author can be concealed, initially at least, this places everyone on an equal standing. Perhaps all attendees could be asked to prepare a 'one-pager' expressing their views on a particular issue as a cost to attending a meeting. Each page could then be shuffled and dealt out before being read to hide the source of the ideas and judge them on their merits alone. Alternatively, 'Brain writing' is a variation on brainstorming in which, instead of debating issues immediately, team members write their views on cards which are posted anonymously on a wall. Any strategy that reduces the influence of deference in judging the quality of an idea will increase the cognitive diversity of the team and the quality of decisions that are taken.

Being proactive in looking outside school for external influences also helps to shake up a comfortable team. It has never been easier to access professional development remotely. Develop an outward-looking ethos that encourages staff to access external influences whilst developing structures, like those above, to bring new thinking back into the school. Why not invite people into your school's wider professional ecosystem through staff reading groups, professional social media clusters or development partnerships with other schools?

Make sure you are making the most of the opportunities presented by being part of a larger structure such as a MAT and that feedback is taken with respect and consideration, even if it is difficult to hear. Encourage staff to contribute to debate through a staff voice system that is given a high priority by senior leaders and leads to tangible changes. Every member of staff needs to be able to express their views without the volunteer's jeopardy of being given extra work or being disparaged as inexperienced with ideas unworthy of attention. If people stop believing their ideas are worthy, they will stop giving them and retreat into their comfort zone.

Becoming T-shaped[26]

Schools, perhaps more than most organisations, often suffer from 'silo' thinking. They divide roles into pastoral or academic which are largely sealed off and separate from each other. Teachers tend to feel comfortable defining themselves as pastorally or academically inclined. Leaders often achieve promotion early in their careers and take on leadership in the pastoral or academic sphere. They then may have little opportunity – or motivation – to broaden their experience. As a result, school organisation structures tend to split into pastoral and academic with little overlap between the two silos.

Teachers in silo schools become 'I-shaped'. A vertical line represents depth without breadth. They have deep knowledge and experience in one area, but rarely have the opportunity to apply these skills in other areas. This will increase stress when I-shaped teachers are asked to operate outside of their comfort zone. It also reduces the effectiveness of teacher teams because it reduces the possibility of challenging the thinking of those who specialise in a different silo of expertise.

This division between pastoral and academic silos is artificial and restrictive. Ideally teachers should have a depth of expertise in their own specialist area, but also breadth of experience across others. This type of teacher is 'T-shaped' with the broad experience represented by a horizontal line that sits on top of the vertical line forming a 'T'. They are likely to be more resilient in operating outside of their comfort zone and more likely to offer alternative perspectives and challenge, thereby increasing a team's cognitive diversity.

A team of t-shaped teachers has greater depth of collective understanding of important issues. Having staff with broad experience also adds collective resilience and provides an insurance policy when experienced personnel leave. In a school which silos its leadership areas, each of the leaders may be an expert in their own area, but have little understanding of, or confidence in, the areas in which their colleagues specialise (Figure 4.5).

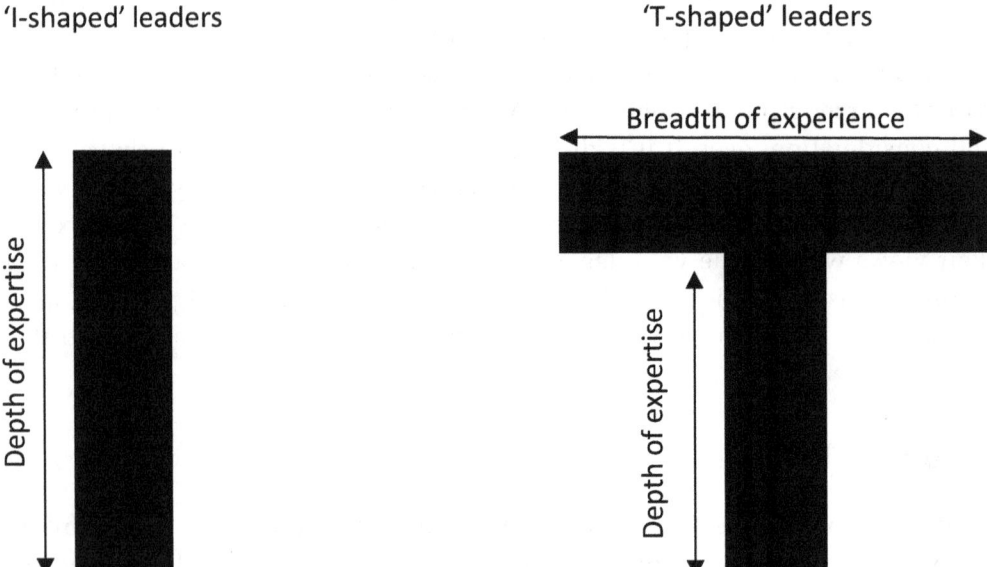

Figure 4.5 The shape of a leader

Create a climate of curiosity

Climate can be difficult to define and therefore create but schools need to develop a culture in which staff are encouraged and rewarded for being professionally curious. Systems should enable colleagues to seek opportunities to push themselves beyond their comfort zones. Seek volunteers or approach people to deliver training and make suggestions for improvement so it's not always the same old faces delivering key messages. Welcome questions and respond promptly. Facilitate role-shadowing and invite staff to sit in on meetings. Don't allow staff to become blinkered to the wider functioning of the school and their place within it.

Every school has its own suite of acronyms and shorthand that are common currency for initiates but bewildering for outsiders. Specialist terms are useful to communicate complex ideas yet can inadvertently exclude those who are not familiar with them. Does everyone in your audience understand what a "LAC" or a "LADO" is? Are you sure that the concept of "blocking" subjects is widely understood within your meeting? It takes a confident individual to ask for clarification in a group setting. Ensure that language is used to illuminate, not obscure, meaning. Always explain specialist terms to encourage wider engagement and broaden staff expertise.

One of the barriers which prevent staff from broadening their experience is job title. Is there any difference between the skills needed to become a pastoral leader and those required to become an academic leader? Both demand flexibility, good planning and organisation, clear communication, empathy, and determination. Chances are that if someone has the skills to become one, they could also do a good job at the other, given time to develop the right knowledge and experience.

Yet names matter. If I identify myself as a "head of year", I may dismiss the idea of being able to lead a subject team, and vice versa. Staff should be involved in reviewing leadership titles. In this process, the discussion is the important part, not the outcomes. You may decide to stay with your existing titles, but by having the conversation, you illuminate the similarities between roles in the pastoral and academic spheres, thereby encouraging staff to diversify their experience. A structure which regularly gives the option for staff to swap responsibilities with others is also useful. Even if no one changes their role, the underlying message is that all roles contribute to the same ultimate value, demand the same skills, and are equally valuable.

Design meetings to mix staff

Make the most of opportunities to mix staff into groups of different roles and levels of responsibility. There is an important place for small and highly focused meetings, but schools need to be careful not to abandon more open forums. Whole-staff meetings are sometimes the only time the staff body meets, yet they are often uninspiring exercises in information giving. Structure discussions that enable staff to gain insight into areas of the school that are less familiar to them. Does an academic leader in your school ever sit down with a pastoral leader and a class teacher to discuss issues that are important to all? If not, make it happen.

Developing leaders is too important to be left to chance, so make it explicit. Does training for ECTs include exposure to pastoral as well as academic issues? Make sure they are given the same weighting. Is there a structured CPD programme for all staff that looks at how to lead from an academic and pastoral background? Capture information about who attends the training and what they're getting out of it, to inform future decision-making.

The best interventions have high impact with low input of time and money. Simple changes in emphasis will embed versatility and create leaders with breadth and depth of experience. For example, be proactive in allowing staff to identify when they need a new challenge before performance dips. A desire for change shouldn't be seen as a failure of resolve, but as a triumph of flexibility. Ultimately, this will broaden your talent pool into the future (Table 4.4) (Figure 4.6).

Dangers of superheroes

If long-term improvement is the goal of schools, they should be rewarded for investing in staff rather than results. Developing T-shaped staff and building structures for ideas to be shared and grow across the organisation are crucial. School improvement is not based on blueprints for success led by omniscient and infallible leaders but by an evolving sense of what principles should be applied to thousands of situations. The most successful organisations come into being and function without anyone having knowledge of the whole. Yet we have built a system which often rewards individuals for their compelling accounts of how they achieved success rather than those who instead recognise the limitations of their knowledge and the importance of the team.

Superhero leaders benefit from the inverse skills problem that can be seen in all large organisations. People at the top of the hierarchy hold great, long-term responsibility but carry relatively light loads of day-to-day decision-making. The closer to the base of an organisational pyramid you look the less long-term responsibility resides but the greater the regularity of daily actions requiring decisiveness. As we established in Chapter 1, actions are easy to measure and quantify. It is relatively easy to assess the actions of a teacher (although hard to do this well). Teachers can be observed during lessons, conclusions can be drawn and quantified. These numerical ratings can then be used to make judgements about competence.

In contrast, leaders spend less time teaching. Their decisions are fewer but with greater impact. However, the impacts of their decisions are more diffuse over time and space. It can be difficult to trace negative outcomes back to any one decision point. Add to this that smart people are highly adept at finding arguments to justify what they wish to be true rather than the correct answer. This situation can

Tilting the table 4.4 T-shaped teams

Contrast the diagram below with the TILT team diagram in Figure 4.4. How does it illustrate the benefits of a team made up of T-shaped leaders?

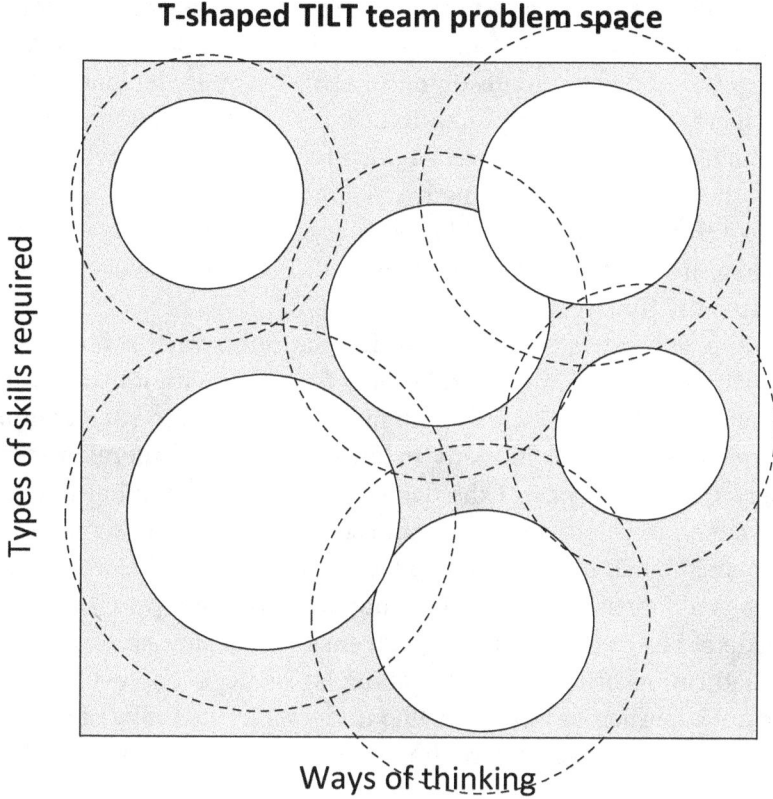

Figure 4.6 T-shaped TILT team

Make a list of three different strategies you will use to develop more T-shaped leaders in your school.

1
2
3

create 'Superhero leaders' who take advantage of the inverse skills problem to self-promote their pivotal role and cement a dominance hierarchy.

Superheroes or survivors?

Football management provides a good illustration of the phenomenon of 'survivors' bias'. Managers have a highly complex role requiring many different skills. For this reason, they are paid high wages and have very poor job security. When results turn, the manager is usually the first to be blamed and lose their jobs. Those that achieve success are lauded by fans and the media, sometimes coming to believe they are 'special'.

However, the reality may be more mundane. There are a limited number of prizes on offer in football so, by definition, most football managers are bound to fail. However, equally certain is the fact that a small number will succeed. Those that succeed are promoted to more prestigious clubs with larger budgets, increasing the chances of success and further promotion. There is a huge amount of randomness in sport, which is part of the reason we love football, but also why no individual can achieve success through their own skill alone. Success means survival and survival can lead to more success, not because of any huge skill of a manager but because someone had to succeed whilst most fail. Football managers are very rarely successful in more than one club.

In education, success is only achieved in relation to other schools so, like football, some schools must succeed, and others fail. At the top of school hierarchies sit leaders who take large decisions with big implications. In such complex organisations, decisions are open to many external factors and therefore randomness. Schools may succeed despite of the decisions leaders take rather than because of them, yet we tend to celebrate people who seem to survive in high office.

Despite being no better or worse than leaders of schools who are deemed to have failed, there is a danger that we assign success to the individual brilliance of superhero leaders. The mundane truth is that sustainable success is built on the hard work and dedication of individuals making small decisions every day. The best leaders are not superheroes but those who understand the limits of their own influence and are able to instead inspire the maximum commitment from their teams.

Conclusions

- Schools cannot succeed without effective teamwork.
- Good teams need people with complimentary skills and experience.
- Members of teams naturally tend to resemble each other over time – this can lead to 'group think' and 'perspective blindness'.
- It is hard to recruit diverse teams in education, so they must be nurtured with existing staff.
- TILT teams are the ideal – they are made up of independent thinkers united by common values to learn and grow together.
- Dominance cultures stifle debate and innovation.
- Prestige cultures cause TILT teams to flourish by fostering authentic relationships and respect.

- Developing T-shaped staff helps to develop cognitive diversity in teams.
- Schools depend on teamwork so we should be sceptical of 'Superhero' leaders.
- Excellent leaders are those who appreciate the limits of their knowledge and inspire commitment in others.

Reference

26 Clemmet, J., 2020. https://www.tes.com/magazine/archived/how-develop-t-shaped-school-leaders.

5 Tilting commitment

The Hunger Games is a book and film franchise in which representatives from different districts of a fictional country are forced to fight each other, once per year, to gain extra food and privileges for themselves and their kinfolk. The spectacle these 'Hunger Games' creates is hugely popular and the winners are feted as heroes.

Similarly, in Roman times, the ruling elites provided 'bread and circuses' to distract the populace from the deprivations of everyday life. Ensuring a supply of grain, and brutal entertainments in the amphitheatre, allowed the ruling class to maintain a status quo. The parallels become clearer once you realise that the name of the country which provides the setting for the Hunger Games is 'panem', meaning 'bread' in Latin. This chapter asks whether some schools today provide 'bread and circuses' for their staff to distract from the worries of everyday life rather than deal with complex, underlying causes of stress.

For example, I once worked with a team to introduce what we called 'well-being weeks' to our programme of regular CPD. Staff hosted a bi-weekly, voluntary workshop on a topic of their choice, from baking to board games, mindfulness to dance. It was well intentioned and, for a time, popular with staff. However, as the weeks passed, and despite initial positive feedback, attendance dwindled. Staff were too tired and hard pressed to commit to anything that was not deemed essential. Given a shortage of time and energy, it was the well-being that went.

Perhaps the problem was that our 'well-being weeks' were the equivalent of 'bread and circuses' for the Roman citizens. Distractions from the everyday problems of making a living in a difficult environment. Without tackling the more complex, underlying issues of the system, such strategies are an irrelevance at best. Well intentioned attempts to improve staff well-being and recognise excellence can be great, but they may be diverting attention from more deep-seated issues that are creating wide-spread anxiety for teachers and students in a broken system. Far better to come up with imaginative ways to operate that do not create as much stress and anxiety in the first place.

This is not a forlorn hope. There are simple ways to make the everyday experience of staff more fulfilling and less challenging without reducing the positive impact on young people's lives. The key is to allow teachers to excel in their key

Tilting the table 5.1 Inspiring motivation

Which of the following factors do you think are the most motivational? Rank them from 1 to 10 according to which is most likely to inspire you to give sustained levels of effort over a long period.

Motivational factor	Rank	Motivational factor	Rank
An increase in wages		Having good work recognised by your line manager	
Good relationships with your line manager		Longer holidays	
Organised socialising with peers		Being nominated for an award by peers	
Being given more time to plan, prepare, and assess lessons		Feeling that your job is secure	
Being asked your opinion and knowing it is valued		Good relationships with peers	

If possible, compare your rankings with a colleague. Discuss the similarities and differences and attempt to explain them.

roles. If we unshackle staff from anxiety and doubt, they will be free to regularly deliver fantastic learning experiences for young people. Well-being weeks and rewards schemes should be welcome additions to, but not irrelevant distractions from, a new caring and empowering educational landscape (Tilting the table 5.1).

Rebellion, compliance, motivation, and commitment

In Chapter 4 we looked at four different groups of colleagues: a Rabble, Clones, Clone Teams, and TILT Teams (Figure 4.3 – Team skills and thinking diversity). A TILT team is one in which individuals have varied experience and diversity of skills and are harmonised by a collective understanding of the values they believe. TILT teams think independently but learn together. Figure 5.1 takes these ideas and illustrates the ways in which groups of rebels can be developed into clone, and eventually TILT, teams.

Evolving a TILT team

Any leader who takes over a rabble knows they have work to do. Perhaps it is a subject team without schemes of work or a year team without a sanctions policy.

72 Tilting commitment

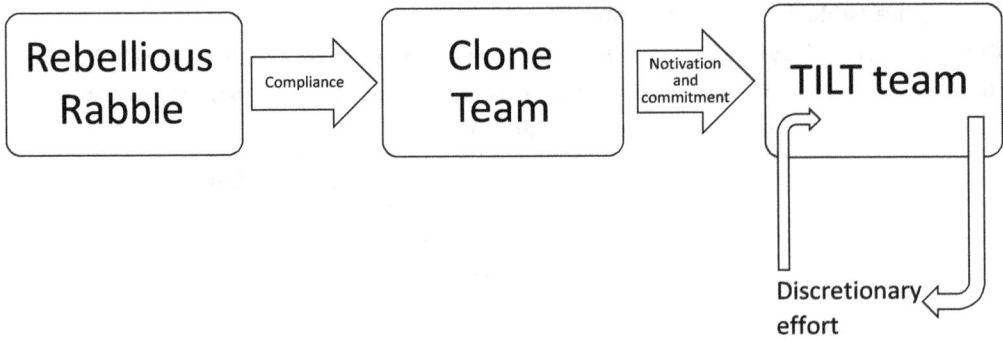

Figure 5.1 Evolving TILT teams

Maybe it is a senior team without a development plan or governors' meeting without agenda. Ultimately, students are being short-changed. This rabble needs clear leadership if rebellion is to be avoided and students get the best schooling possible.

In such a situation, compliance is necessary. Without coordinated working it will be impossible to unify standards and ensure equitable access to high-quality education for all. Documents and policies are required. Teaching and learning strategies need to be agreed. Assessment needs to be standardised and checking protocols put in place to make sure that everyone is doing as they should.

This requires robust and well-organised leadership. Difficult conversations are needed, and teachers held to account. Policies need to be clear and seen to be carried out to retain credibility. Compliance is not a short-term project and should not be underestimated. The result will be moving your team from a rabble to a clone team. It will take a toll on leaders and teachers, but ultimately it will benefit students and is necessary.

Clone teams are organised. They operate systems and follow protocols that are well established and understood. Rebels have either learned to comply or they have chosen somewhere else to work. Learning walks reveal lessons that are standardised, planning samples show uniformity in marking and book samples tell of students making the same progress in all classes.

Unfortunately, compliance is necessary for success, but it is not sufficient. After a while, staff tire, leaders become jaded, and the team just want the holidays to arrive. Attending a baking club after school might(?!) be fun but it won't relieve the exhaustion. Compliance is necessary, but not sufficient to build a team that can deliver sustainable success. In the long term, teachers need to be inspired to think independently and coordinated by shared values which help them learn together: a TILT team.

Two-state model

TILT teams are characterised by staff who give discretionary effort, or 'go the extra mile'. These are staff who do more than merely what they must. People giving discretionary effort turn a good team into a great team.

American psychologist Frederick Herzberg proposed a helpful two-state model for motivating commitment in the workplace.[25] He categorised factors that actively motivate workers and those that are neutral unless they are removed. For example, being involved in decision-making, receiving recognition for one's work, and feeling that your contribution is meaningful are 'motivators' that encourage commitment to a cause. In contrast, factors such as good pay, job security, and paid holidays are 'hygiene' factors that are taken for granted unless they are taken away or eroded.

The problem with clone teams is that they reduce individual decision-making. Standardised approaches proliferate in many schools and academy trusts, which erode the autonomy of individual teachers and teams. Performing as expected is the primary virtue of standardisation and this removes personal agency, rendering work unrewarding. At the same time, austerity has created a double whammy as security of pay and conditions are threatened both in perception and reality. The erosion of these, and other hygiene factors, removes certainty and reduces motivation.

Perhaps a first step to combat this double jeopardy is to look again at clone teams. A certain amount of coordination is essential, but not at the cost of staff feeling able to contribute to decision-making. We need some of that rebellious, independent spirit to be retained in our clone teams so that teachers remain motivated. Perhaps developing shared long- and medium-term plans is essential, but teachers should be able to interpret these plans in their own way during lessons. Maybe agreeing types of assessment is non-negotiable but deciding when and exactly how these will be used is left to individuals.

Interestingly, according to Herzberg, offering more money or longer holidays is unlikely to improve motivation. Herzberg considered the most important hygiene factors to be the level of supervision worked under, as well as good relationships with bosses and peers. Paradoxically, it seems that in our marketised system, performance-related pay is less important for motivation than making staff feel valued and secure (Tilting the table 5.2).

Motivation and commitment

There is a useful distinction to be drawn between motivation and commitment. Motivations are driven by emotion, and commitment by self-will. For example, the original motivations for getting together with your life partner may be physical attraction, shared interests, or a sense of humour. However, there will be times during a long and successful relationship when these original motivations fade or disappear completely. It is at these times that commitment preserves a relationship. Deciding to stick with a decision even when we don't feel like it differentiates long-term commitment from daily motivation.

At work, well-designed staff recognition systems, or well-being policies may increase motivation for a time but, even for the most dedicated professional, it is

Tilting the table 5.2 Returning to motivation
Re-read the factors you ranked earlier. Which do you think Herzberg would count as motivational and which as hygiene factors?

Motivational factor	Motivational or hygiene?	Motivational factor	Motivational or hygiene?
An increase in wages		Having good work recognised by your line manager	
Good relationships with your line manager		Longer holidays	
Organised socialising with peers		Being nominated for an award by peers	
Being given more time to plan, prepare, and assess lessons		Feeling that your job is secure	
Being asked your opinion and knowing it is valued		Good relationships with peers	

Are some factors more important than others for motivating you in the long term?

impossible to feel motivated (emotionally engaged) all day, every day. Figure 5.2 shows shifts in motivation for a member of staff over several years. This will be based on a variety of motivation, hygiene, and personal factors and fluctuates widely. The commitment line, however, acts as a base line or safety net below which discretionary effort will not fall. Even when motivation is low, commitment remains high and consistent.

It is important to understand the factors that will increase both motivation (short-term emotional buy-in) and commitment (intellectual buy-in) if discretionary effort is to be maximised. The degree and type of supervision, as well as good relationships with bosses and peers are the most important factors in developing motivation and commitment. These should therefore be our focus when building long-term commitment to a team and its values.

Inspiring motivation and commitment

Leadership skills fall into more than one category. Good leaders need to have specific knowledge of the technical skills which are crucial for the activity they lead. It helps if school leaders are evidently good teachers or good with students. Although at senior leadership level these skills are a small part of daily life, being experienced at them gives leaders credibility.

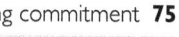

Figure 5.2 Motivation and commitment

On a more conceptual level, it is important for leaders to be able to understand and be able to manipulate abstract concepts and ideas, so that they can plan strategically for the future. It is impossible to implement a vision, no matter how brilliant, if leaders don't understand how timetables, schemes of work, or assessment policies, for example, work.

The most important set of skills that leaders need, however, are people skills. Successful leaders are able to show their humanity consistently through their daily behaviour. The type of person you are, is far more important for motivating others than your brilliant organisational skills or stunning vision for your team. If you develop your personal skills and demonstrate them in an authentic manner, consistently over time, you will motivate others, building commitment and inspiring discretionary effort.

Epoché and empathy

Empathy, putting yourself in the shoes of others, is key to good leadership. When listening to the concerns of others or considering implementing a change of policy, leaders must be able to understand and anticipate problems from the perspective of others. However, to be truly effective, leaders need to display epoché as well as empathy.

Epoché means suspending judgement about something, or someone. In pressurised environments, school leaders are used to making decisions quickly. Being decisive is an important skill and understanding how others will react helps with this. Sometimes, however, it is easier to rush to a conclusion because time is tight, rather than withholding judgement and taking more time to think things through.

Sometimes leaders fear admitting that they find things difficult to decide. However, it shows far more humanity, to be open about the complexity of an issue and the importance of a variety of views. The strategies outlined in Chapter 4, for widening the diversity of voices in team meetings, provide practical ways to gather these views. However, just allowing contrasting opinions to be aired is an empty gesture if our pre-conceived ideas are set too hard.

If your mind is already made up, or your opinion of someone has been formed before an issue is aired, putting yourself in their shoes will just confirm your prejudice. Leaders need to be able to clear their minds and judge each case or person on their merits every time. Epoché is akin not just to putting yourself in the shoes of others and imagining what it would be like. It is also walking around in them for a while, even if you develop blisters or dislike the style. Empathising with others, even those with whom you share little in common, and being prepared to change your mind, is the skill of epoché (Tilting the table 5.3).

We are (not) family

When describing their team, a dedicated colleague may say 'we are like a family'. This sounds positive, conjuring up images of shared conversations over a meal, investment in each other's personal lives, and fierce loyalty. However, whilst genuine dialogue, showing an interest and loyalty are important, they can also be problematic. If we are not careful, a family culture can harm the development of TILT teams which are honestly combined in the pursuit of improvement.

Families are defined by the permanent bonds of love that tie members together. It is their most significant feature, and yet when replicated in a professional team this structure can be corrosive. Just as in a family, fear of upsetting relationships may cause colleagues to suppress difficult conversations in the interests of preserving harmony. Family disagreements may be papered over because of the infrequency of contact and the high stakes involved. However, professional bonds need to be both more flexible and more robust. They will be tested daily in pressured situations and, unlike in families, professional bonds can easily be broken.

To develop strong, but flexible, team bonds a culture of 'honesty' needs to be developed. Too often we call conversations 'difficult'; usually what we mean is

Tilting the table 5.3 Developing epoché

1. Have you ever discounted an idea because of who it came from rather than how good it was? If you feel able, share this with a trusted colleague.
2. Think of someone you find it difficult to empathise with and consider how you could better get to know what makes them tick – share your ideas with a trusted colleague.

If you find it difficult to resist making a quick decision, script a response to use before you make a final choice. For example: 'We're not going to solve this now, let's all have a think and come back to it in our next meeting'.

honest. I don't know anyone who is naturally good at taking feedback, so teams need to proactively practice giving and receiving honest feedback and praise. Modelling your own struggles and disappointments will help, as well as listening to feedback from colleagues in a positive manner.

It can be uncomfortable to be told that you've done something well and it is really hard to hear that you could have done something better. Plan delivering praise and critique to maximise the impact of both.

Giving good news

We all like to hear good news about ourselves. Experiments have shown that, even when we receive praise we know it is insincere, it improves our mood. Con artists and lotharios have exploited this human failing for centuries. However, there are ways of delivering a compliment which motivate and other ways that have minimal, or even negative, impact.

Some leaders believe that praise should be difficult to gain, but its value doesn't decline with use. If you withhold praise when it is due, you run the risk of increasing anxiety in the team and encouraging manipulative behaviours from team members who compete to receive a rare word of approval. Be free with your praise.

Having said this, delivering praise when it is not due is counterproductive. People are very good at spotting when you are being authentic and will cease to notice false praise. The same is true if you add a negative attachment to your praise. Don't follow a compliment with 'but', instead use 'and'. For example instead of, 'thank you for challenging that student about littering, but please don't shout', try 'thank you for challenging that student and would you do things the same way next time?'. Praise needs to be precise, so seize the moment and praise as soon as you see something praiseworthy occur (but be aware that some like public praise and others prefer private).

Receiving bad news

No one likes receiving bad news so there are a few things we can do to make it easier for someone to hear. For example, giving time and space between an event and giving feedback. Allowing someone to calm and reflect on an incident, if appropriate and possible, is likely to allow them perspective and to gain a clearer view. Ask them for their opinion before giving yours and separate the person from their behaviour or performance. Use phrases such as 'I agree that … and I want to check what you mean by ….'

Make sure you check back with someone after the dust has settled. You may need to be more direct if they have not heard the message you thought you were delivering. Remember, this is an honest conversation not a difficult one. The goal is to improve things for students, so it is important to get it right. The aim is not punishment but improvement.

Make sure that you have allocated enough time and avoid either running over or having to rush. Also, think about where the discussion should take place. Is it better to choose a neutral space or go to them? It can sometimes be difficult to end a conversation in your own space if people fail to read non-verbal cues. If you meet in their environment, it is easier to end the interaction as you can choose when to leave.

Body language is important, as is your tone and intonation. There are no hard and fast rules but stating that your agenda is to help and not to judge is a useful place to start the meeting.

Equally important as giving honest feedback is receiving it. If we become defensive, colleagues will quickly realise that a door may be open for feedback, but they need to put a hard hat on before they go through it. Remember not to mix up personal with professional feedback and recognise that it takes bravery to deliver a hard message. The deliverer may be nervous, even if they are superior to you in the leadership structure, so thank them for the feedback, ask for clarification, and make a note of what they say. A message may become garbled so make sure you are totally clear about the issue, perhaps read your notes back to your colleague to check. If you disagree with the feedback say so, but with tact. Ask for some time to consider the conversation.

Try to view all feedback as a gift. After taking some time, you may realise that, even if you don't agree with everything said, there are some grains of truth which you can use to improve your performance and that of those around you. Find the elements of truth and show initiative in implementing changes to address these issues. Don't forget to go back to the messenger of your feedback and let them know what you are doing and why you are doing it. This approach turns a potentially damaging encounter into a growth encounter for both parties (Table 5.4).

Go with the flow

Have you ever experienced 'flow'? The term was first coined by mihaly csikszentmihalyi, an American psychologist to describe the sense of effortless action you feel when engrossed in a task that is just about manageable. I have occasionally felt it for (very) short moments when playing the piano or painting water colours. One becomes so involved in the activity that you lose track of time and self. Sports people, actors, and musicians often talk about experiencing this state, but it is just as common when completing a crossword puzzle, crocheting, or teaching.

When we experience flow, it feels like we have been transported to a higher state of being. We perform at the height of our powers and operate almost unconsciously. When teaching you may feel the class hanging on your words, know exactly who to ask what type of question to, when to speed up and when to slow down. These are the lessons when the students are surprised when the bell goes and leave the class still discussing the lesson.

Teaching is a performance. To achieve flow, like an actor or dancer about to take to the stage, teachers need to develop routines to clear their minds and focus their

Tilting the table 5.4 Giving and receiving feedback

Think of times that you have delivered praise and critique. Which of the following do you think are the most important tips to remember? Give each a score out of five.

Giving praise	Importance /5	Giving critique	Importance /5
Be free with praise		Leave a time delay	
Avoid false praise		Ask for their opinion first	
Avoid praise with attachments		Separate the person from the behaviour	
Be precise		Check back later to clarify the message	
Seize the moment		Allocate enough time	
Think whether private or public is best		Choose the location carefully	

Compare your scores with a colleague and discuss similarities and differences. Talk about times when giving positive, or negative, feedback has gone well or badly – why was this?

attention. This is difficult enough but can be more complicated when one lesson follows hard on the heels of another. These could be different topics, year groups and even in different parts of the school, but no allowance is made. Lessons are rightly expected to start crisply, engage students quickly, and maintain purposeful pace throughout.

As with sport or the arts, developing simple breathing or mindfulness routines can prepare your mind for flow. There are many examples of these which you could try out. Generally, however, they focus on removing sources of unhelpful stress, recognising the signs of increasing stress and dealing with these symptoms when they occur to keep stress within ideal parameters.

Arousing peak performance

In sporting terms, the dangers that unhelpful stress creates are called 'under arousal', or 'over arousal' (Figure 5.3). A certain amount of stress is crucial for performance levels. If a sports star takes to the field too relaxed they will be 'under aroused'. They will be ill prepared and lethargic. They may be caught cold and lose ground in a contest which is difficult to regain. It is not uncommon to see sports people hitting and slapping themselves to raise their level of arousal before competition begins.

If this goes too far, however, competitors could become over aroused. With too much stress in their system, a runner or swimmer may set off too quickly and run out of energy before the finishing line or a boxer may be spent after an opening flourish of punches, leaving them exhausted and exposed to a sucker punch.

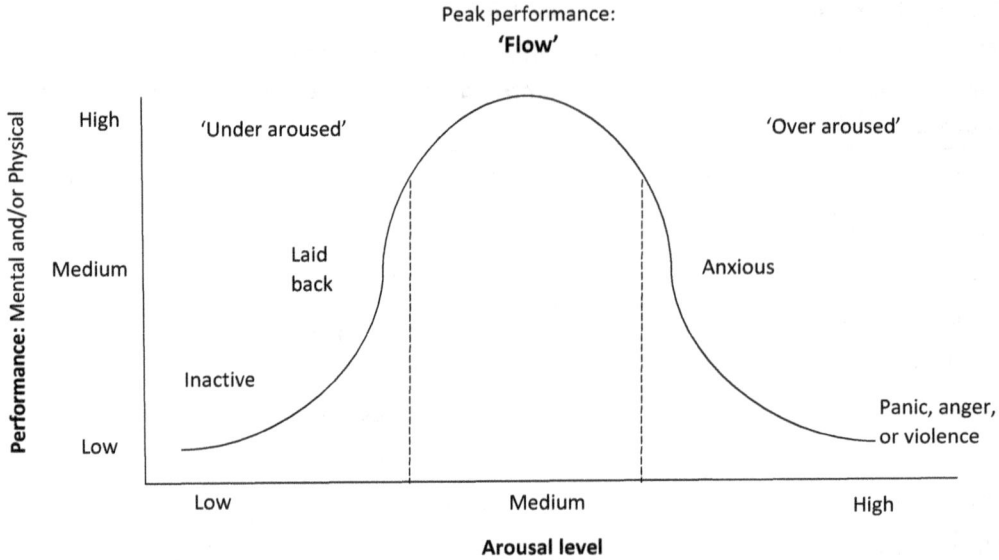

Figure 5.3 Performance curve

In terms of teaching, the best lessons will be taught when teachers experience 'flow' in the classroom. For this to be possible they need to be able to control their level of stress to maintain a medium arousal level (Figure 5.3). Too low and lessons will lack pace and engagement. Too high and lessons become frenetic, teachers and students become over-stressed and exhausted. For this reason, the main job of leadership in schools needs to be focused on eliminating arousal drains and enhancing circumstances to calm over arousal. Maximising the occurrence of 'flow' in our classrooms is the best way to accelerate student progress. All leadership efforts should therefore recognise this as their principal aim.

Arousal drains

Many of us will have studied Maslow's hierarchy of needs as part of our teacher training (Figure 5.4). This theory postulates that students need their physical and emotional needs to be met before they can be expected to learn. However, how many of us apply the theory to staff as well as students? Just like pupils, teachers need to feel secure if they are to feel settled, achieve flow, and inspire great learning in the classroom.

Arousal drains proliferate if teachers don't feel secure. Leaders need to ensure structural measures which build physical and organisational security. Do staff have their own rooms and access to their own resources where possible? Are people's roles and responsibilities clear and differentiated from others? Does everyone know and understand the protocols which lubricate the school day? These factors need to be ensured by leaders. If staff are to be unencumbered by doubt and anxiety and perform at the peak of their powers their physical and psychological security needs to be the priority.

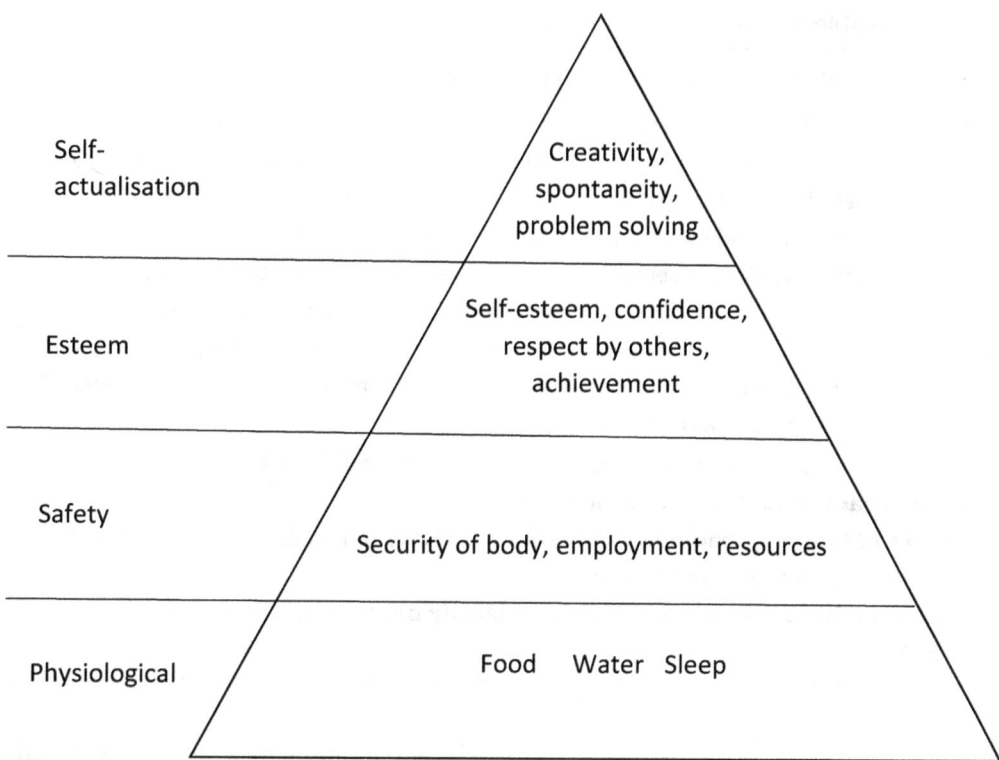

Figure 5.4 Maslow's hierarchy of needs

There are several common arousal drains to watch out for. For example, poor student behaviour and lack of a clear behaviour policy can demoralise staff, draining their ability to perform. In addition, we have already looked at the negative influence of bogus quantification on staff morale. When any number, sometimes based on the flimsiest of data, is better than the qualitative judgements of experienced professionals it can be disheartening, draining motivation.

Professional trust is crucial in maintaining motivation and commitment. Trust is built in the long term but can collapse quickly if leaders are not alert. Oversight is important, but good staff need to be given the freedom to innovate, and potentially fail, if improvements are to be made. Be careful not to make quality assurance so invasive that it inspires safe practice or a 'speed camera' mentality. Staff may be incentivised to replicate expected behaviours only when observed if they are not personally committed to these behaviours. When unsupervised they will revert to rebellious behaviour unless oversight is seen as a collaborative and developmental process (Tilting the table 5.5).

One of the best teachers I ever worked with built brilliant relationships with their students, had expert subject knowledge and helped them achieve great results. This fabulous teacher was also perpetually anxious that they were not 'doing it right' (i.e. conforming to the protocols for teaching laid down in the official policy). This made lesson observations an ordeal for them.

Tilting the table 5.5 How useful are your lesson observations?

Read the following summary of an experiment.

Videos of paramedics in action were shown to invited audiences, some experienced paramedics, some laypeople, and some teachers of paramedic science. Surprisingly, when asked to distinguish the novice paramedics from the experienced staff, using the video evidence, the laypeople and experienced paramedics were more successful than the teachers of paramedic skills. It seems that the teachers judged expertise by adherence to the rules which they taught. They saw such conformity more often in the novices and mistook it for expertise. Laypeople and experienced paramedics valued confidence, decisiveness and results above following agreed protocols and were more likely to identify the most experienced and well-respected paramedics successfully.[27]

- Do you think it is more important for teachers to follow agreed protocols or to be proactive and adapt to circumstance?
- Can good teaching happen, even when teachers fail to follow your agreed protocols for lesson observation?
- Does your lesson observation policy identify protocols, successful teaching, or both?

There should be room for conclusions to be accepted even when they can only be incompletely justified through observation. It should be acceptable to judge that outcomes are good even if the 'right' actions are not observed, even if there is no common agreement about how or why those outcomes are achieved. It is possible for a lesson to be brilliant, even if it is not possible to tick all the necessary boxes on the observation form. To insist otherwise is to be a slave to protocol.

Agreed structures for teaching lessons are necessary but not sufficient to motivate and inspire experienced teachers. Once the rules become second nature, teachers should be free to use their experience and skill to deviate, or even subvert them, in pursuit of pupil engagement and progress. This is the real professional trust which helps teachers flourish and continue improving throughout their careers.

Virtue signalling

'Virtue signalling' has a severe deleterious impact on staff motivation and commitment. This term, meaning publicly expressing information intended to demonstrate one's good character, have become part of the English language over the last ten years or so. They are illustrated in staff rooms up and down the country by members of staff who needlessly broadcast how many hours of marking they do or how guilty they feel about taking days off during school holidays. Teaching is hard enough without colleagues making you feel guilty if your laptop sometimes stays at school or you leave work before being thrown out by the site staff.

Thankfully, the Department of Education recognise the dangerous correlation that some staff make between how many hours a colleague works and how good a teacher they are. In their excellent working report 'Reducing unnecessary workload around marking' the Independent Teacher Workload Review Group helpfully note that "The quantity of feedback should not be confused with the quality. The quality of the feedback, however given, will be seen in how a pupil is able to tackle subsequent work".[28] Change your culture if necessary, from validating workaholic attitudes to seeing them as dangers to mental health. This encourages more focussed and less time-consuming practice which benefits staff and therefore students.

Would it not be great if some of the most influential staff in your school were known for their commitment to friends and family. If they were respected for teaching great lessons as well as having a sustainable social life. Good teachers need to have their own hobbies as well as leading extracurricular activities. Exceptional staff need healthy private relationships as well as caring, professional relationships with students. This is not an either / or, but a both / also scenario. When staff have both a secure life balance and a sustainable work schedule it is better for students. All benefit when staff are content and well-rested for the classroom.

Dealing with emotion

When levels of arousal become too high the unwanted result can be panic, anger, or violence (Figure 5.3) and the same can be true in schools. As a school leader, we often work in volatile situations with young people who find it difficult to regulate their own behaviour. This may manifest as students who are loud, disrespectful, or overly physical. Whilst the same behaviours will hopefully be rarely seen amongst staff, it is important to recognise the signs in oneself and others that unhelpful levels of stress are affecting behaviour with negative consequences.

There are three reactions to stress in the natural world: fight, freeze, or flight. Although physical altercations between staff should never occur, the fight response can take other more subtle guises. Aggression may take the form of verbal outbursts and obstructive argumentation. Colleagues may canvass support amongst colleagues and try to create cliques around themselves of people who share their views. It is important to understand that behaviour communicates what is going on in someone's mind. Although it can be hard, it is vital not to react to these fight behaviours with emotional responses of your own. Understanding and addressing the underlying emotion will allow you to unpick the behaviour and deal with the root cause.

For those whose natural stress response is freeze or flight the corresponding behaviours in school may be to ignore requests, avoid addressing issues, change the subject, side-track conversations, and passively resist taking responsibility.

Stressed colleagues may even resort to duplicity, trying to shift blame to others, and even push it back to you. In these situations it can be easy to be drawn into investigations of facts rather than remembering that behaviours are symptoms of fundamental issues. Lack of psychological or organisational security create stress which causes the actions we observe. Instead of reacting to behaviour, tease out the causes of stress which drive the behaviours.

Firstly, use epoché to allow any emotional response to be shown without judging the individual. Make it clear that emotion is a positive trait, although strategies for controlling it will help resolve issues more quickly in the future. Next, once emotion has subsided, ask open questions to show empathy and start to build a picture of the underlying causes of emotion. Make notes which you can then use at your next scheduled encounter to summarise issues without reviving the emotions of your earlier meeting.

When it all goes wrong

You may have read the preceding passage and had the cynical thought that it all sounds very simple on paper. You work in incredibly pressured environments, and it is not always easy to remain detached. It can be tempting to be drawn into argument and it can be easy to be seduced by the need to have the last word. For this reason, it is important to have strategies for when you feel yourself losing self-control.

Firstly, learn to recognise the physiological signs that your levels of stress are becoming unhelpful. Maybe your heart beats faster, your breath grows short, or you face begins to change colour. Whatever it might be, as soon as you feel it, bring a warning word to the front of your mind. It could be 'pause', 'stop', or something a little more earthy. As soon as the word flashes across your mind begin your stress protocol.

Imagine that you are watching drone footage of yourself. Ask yourself how important this scene will be in the movie of your life when it is inevitably made. Once you realise that it is unlikely to make the final cut you can take some practical steps to improve your situation.

Firstly, explain that you are going to take some time to make your next response in the exchange and then use that time to plan. Assess what you can change immediately about the interaction and what you have to accept and work with. Your aim is to bring the encounter to a swift conclusion without having made any commitments, or said anything, you will later regret. Committing an exit line to memory can help when your emotions are running high. For example, 'thank you for your views, I will take time to think and come back to you'.

Finally, once the immediate situation is resolved and you have time to reflect, try to laugh at yourself. If you have over-reacted, try to see the lighter side and smile. It is unlikely that any long-term damage has been done so take some time out away from email. This is to avoid the temptation for an 'esprit d'escalier', a

Tilting the table 5.6 Make a plan
Make a plan to motivate your team.
Use the table below to help:

Aim	Actions	Who, by when?
Building compliance		
Building motivation (short term) and commitment (long term)		
Showing epoché		
Giving praise better		
Giving and receiving critique		
Eliminating arousal drains		
Encouraging flow		

French phrase meaning 'wit of the staircase'. It refers to the remark that occurs to a person after the opportunity to make it has passed. If you are close to a keyboard you may be drawn into an email esprit d'escalier which will only make things worse. Let things lie (Tilting the table 5.6).

Conclusions

- Staff and student well-being are essential, not just nice to have.
- Treating the symptoms of anxiety and stress with well-being events is good but not enough on its own.
- Anxiety and stress are undesirable symptoms of poor systems and behaviours – change the system to address the causes, not just the symptoms.
- Compliance is a necessary, but not sufficient, trait of TILT teams that succeed.
- Good relationships with bosses and peers are the main motivators of discretionary effort.
- Consistent motivational structures and behaviours build long-term commitment.
- Epoché and empathy enable leaders to have effective truthful conversations that lead to sustainable improvement.
- All leadership efforts should be aimed at increasing the incidence of 'flow' in the classroom.
- Arousal drains need to be identified and eliminated to encourage peak performance in the classroom.
- When dealing with emotional responses identify the underlying causes.
- Be prepared if you lose control of your emotions.

References

27 Herzberg, F., Mausner, B., and Snyderman, B.B., 1959. *The motivation to work* (2nd ed.). John Wiley. ISBN 0471373893.
28 https://assets.publishing.service.gov.uk/government/uploads/system/uploads/attachment_data/file/511256/Eliminating-unnecessary-workload-around-marking.pdf

6 Tilting problems

My favourite children's book is called 'The Giant Jam Sandwich'.[29] I loved it as a child and have loved reading it to my own children. In the tale, the small village of Itching Down is invaded by a plague of wasps. The leader, Mayor Muddlenut, calls a meeting in the village hall and asks the people for ideas. Despite an initial lack of good suggestions, a plan is eventually hatched to bake and construct a giant jam sandwich in which to trap the wasps. All ends well. The rhymes are great and the pictures entrancing for children.

Like most good works of literature, however, there are several layers to the story. The author pokes fun at the pomposity of grownups, the hierarchies of adult life and the certainties of 'big idea' thinking. This is thinking which involves finding a simple, grand solution to a problem. If properly implemented, the 'big idea' will resolve all issues and people can live happily ever after. It is common in children's fables, where 'love's true kiss' or the 'one ring to rule them all' underpin exciting tales of good triumphing over evil. However, in the real world, 'big ideas' can be problematic.

My impression is that the authors of 'The Giant Jam Sandwich', understand this. The book is exposing the naïve certainty with which we often approach difficult issues, and by doing so undermines it. Usually there is no 'big idea' solution, but we like the simplicity of believing in the big idea anyway. Faith in the big idea persists longer than it should. The logic runs that if something has not worked so far it is because we have not done it either long enough or consistently enough or people are just not doing it right.

Modernism and the power of big ideas

The Giant Jam Sandwich was written in the 1970s, when two big ideas dominated the world: Communism in the East and Capitalism in the West. Both philosophies were underpinned by faith that, if left to operate without hindrance, these ideas would eventually create ideal societies. This was the age of 'Modernism'. From automated factories and inner-city redevelopments in the West, to the grand building

Tilting the table 6.1 Big ideas in education

Mayor Muddlenut wanted a 'big idea' to rid his village of wasps. What big ideas have you come across in education and how would you rate their success? (some possible examples have been supplied). Discuss your answers with a colleague.

Big Idea	Rating (1 = Highly Effective, 3 = No effect, 5 = Damaging)
Three-part lessons (the idea that lessons should be divided into three distinct sections – Starter, Main, and Plenary – common in the 2000s)	
Yellow box marking/Triple Marking (the idea that the most effective marking involved a written dialogue between student and teacher – common in the 2010s)	
Retrieval practice (the idea that in order to embed learning in the long-term memory, lessons should contain regular recaps of previously learned content – common in the 2020s)	

---

projects and collectivisation of the East, people trusted that 'big idea' thinking would eventually save the world.

Since then, however, the world has moved on. Many big ideas have been discredited and we are now more commonly said to be in a 'post-modern' world in which diversity, nimbleness, and flexibility are seen as the most effective ways to solve problems. Rapid technological development and innovation have driven eye watering change in society and the economy. However, the world of education moves slowly.

It is easy to be seduced by the idea that problems faced by schools can be solved only if we can find the right 'big idea'. Solutions that work in one school or location are seized upon and spread rapidly through the system. Lack of time or energy to develop ideas encourages schools to limit themselves to ensuring compliance with whichever big idea is currently in vogue. Rather than adopt and adapt new ideas, too often we accept them and devote our limited resources to ensuring compliance. This is Mayor Muddlenut thinking (Tilting the table 6.1).

Bicycles for all

Let us imagine a school who canvassed their disadvantaged students for ideas to support them in their learning. A creative and committed leader spoke to a boy and asked why they were regularly coming to school late. It transpired that the boy had a long walk which, added to caring responsibilities at home, often delayed his departure for school. The leader had a great idea. Why not use Pupil Premium funding to buy the boy a bike? It was not easy to persuade the head teacher, but eventually an agreement was made, the bike was purchased, and the boy's attendance improved dramatically.

This is a great example of a 'post-modern' mindset at work. Being nimble, respecting diversity and implementing a bespoke solution. Unfortunately, the story does not end there.

At the next meeting of the MAT middle leadership group, the leader (let's call her Louise), was invited to talk about the bike idea. Louise is a charismatic leader and enthused the group with her story. It had a particularly profound impact on Kevin, a year leader from another school. He returned and told the story to his disadvantaged lead, who told the story to Sam, the head teacher. With the pressure of an imminent Ofsted inspection and data showing poor disadvantaged performance, Sam was decisive and immediately ordered new bikes for every one of their eighty-nine Year 11 disadvantaged pupils.

This was Mayor Muddlenut thinking. A solution that worked well somewhere else was grasped and immediately applied in a different context. Only 20% of the bikes were still owned by a pupil a year later, the school massively overspent its Pupil Premium budget and there was no improvement in the progress (or attendance) of disadvantaged students.

The virtues of obliquity

Developing obliquity is a way to combat 'big idea' thinking. Obliquity means approaching problems from an angle ('obliquely') rather than directly.[30] This contrasts with the 'direct' approach favoured by Muddlenuts everywhere.

Direct problem solvers start with a small number of possible solutions to an issue. Then, having made a choice, they doggedly implement their solution. Tenacity and resilience are their chief virtues, however, there are at least a couple of drawbacks to this approach. It presupposes that we have all the information we need to understand what an appropriate solution might look like. Also, having made our choice, it relies on circumstances remaining the same so that our decision retains its relevance. Neither of these are necessarily, nor even usually, true in schools.

In contrast, oblique decision makers make an initial decision followed by regular reviews and new choices based on the range of options that open up as a situation develops. This is termed 'Successive Limited Comparison'.[31] To be an oblique leader means knowing the limitations of your knowledge from the start and making decisions accordingly. Choices are contingent on circumstances, which can be highly dynamic in school environments. Previous choices are regularly revisited, re-evaluated, and open to adaptation and change. Flexibility and lateral thinking are the key virtues.

Schools need nimble thinkers who hold consistent shared values, as well as stubborn thinkers who enforce consistent actions. The people who genuinely transform schools are those who repeatedly adapt and innovate whilst reinforcing communally held values; not Muddlenuts, who plough on with their dogmatic agenda, bulldozing dissent and eliminating challenge along the way.

Obliquity works

Oblique leaders recognise their dependence on the actions of a hugely diverse collective of individuals within their organisation. These individuals are largely unaware of their potential impact on the whole and the system is too complex to effectively supervise them from the centre. Instead of surveillance and enforcement, oblique leaders in all fields prioritise a collective understanding and commitment to shared values.

For example, great art is created by those who value art, not income. Whether it generates acclaim or revenue is a secondary consideration. When a successful film director first meets a screen writer, they don't talk about how the script could be adapted to increase its commercial appeal; this is not the main value. Instead, they ask, "What is the story about? What did you see? What was your intention? ... what do you hope the audience will feel, think, sense? In what mood do you want to them to leave the theatre?"[32] They understand that when a film meets its artistic aims, box office success is more likely to follow.

Similarly (and contrary to common belief) brilliant businesses are not built by people trying to maximise profit at all costs. Multi-billionaires rightly receive their fair share of criticism, but people like Elon Musk, Steve Jobs, and Jeff Bezos rarely set out solely to become rich – if they did they would be unlikely to succeed in the long term. Successful entrepreneurs have great ideas for innovations, and passion for their product or service which they can communicate compellingly to others. However, Google, Amazon, and the rest, have changed and adapted over time as the environment they operate in has evolved. None of their visionary leaders have doggedly pursued a single end from the beginning; instead, they have switched and flexed, overseeing major changes in their products and services whilst inspiring their organisations, and without compromising their values.

In all successful organisations, including schools, the only constant is the commitment to a set of ideals. The former president of multi-national pharmaceutical company Merck and Co puts it like this, "We try never to forget that medicine is for the people. It is not for profit. The profits follow, and if we have remembered that they have never failed to appear".[33]

Franklin's gambit

Most of us think that we find solutions to problems by weighing up the pros and cons. Often we will write, or imagine, a list of the benefits and drawbacks of a course of action and make what we think is a rational decision. This is a process known, by a phrase first coined by Benjamin Franklin, as 'moral algebra'.

However, although he popularised the process, Franklin understood that moral algebra often only provides an illusion of rational decision-making. He put it like this: "So convenient a thing it is to be a reasonable creature, since it enables one to find or make a reason for everything one had a mind to do".[34] In other words, we manipulate our thinking to favour the solution we wanted all along. In schools, for example, we devote great time and energy to appraisal and quality assurance processes that are consistent and reliable. However, in truth, are we sometimes simply filling in forms to validate judgements already made and based on other criteria entirely?

Neat problem-solving using a moral algebra approach seems sensible but is problematic. Identifying costs and benefits requires us to understand a problem and know at least one possible solution before we start. However, schools are too complex for individuals to fully understand, and the consequences of what we do depend on multiple responses we cannot predict. We also have many objectives which are often, at least partly, incompatible and we seldom have all the information about the problem that we need before we start.

We should be sceptical, therefore, of any school leader who gives definitive advice on solutions to anything but the simplest problems. Even the best advice is likely merely to be based on partial reasons for their own past success, retrospective rationalisations rather than explanations. Such leaders may be unaware of, or unlikely to acknowledge, the role of chance or context in their triumphs and, if not treated with caution, such advice can be dangerous. Instead, solutions emerge through experimentation; getting on with the job every day, motivated by strong shared values but without following any grand design or eminent other (Table 6.2).

What's the problem?

It is too easy to kid ourselves that we lead in schools by making rational decisions based on objective data or 'expert' judgements. This downplays and seeks to deny the vital role of professional intuition. In many cases, whether a complete explanation for a path of action can be articulated is not as important as whether we collectively agree on its suitability. This does not mean acting on unsubstantiated hunches, but high-quality intuition based on years of experience. Academic, Cass Sunstein, terms policies based on expert intuition, 'Incompletely theorised agreements'.[35] They are based on experimentation and review interpreted through experience and discussion. In busy schools, incompletely theorised agreements lie at the heart of the decision-making process, even if they may be disguised as moral algebra.

Thinking that schools are improved solely by pursuing well-defined goals, broken down into actions whose progress can be neatly measured denies reality. Action plans are necessary but are not sufficient to establish great schools. Embracing the fact that

Tilting the table 6.2 Moral algebra and Franklin's gambit

Read these two examples of moral algebra and Franklin's gambit in use. Come up with an example when you have used moral algebra to solve an issue in school. How much of your final decision was based on moral algebra (weighing up the pros and cons to make a rational decision) and how much on Franklin's gambit (using moral algebra as a cover to enable one to find, or make, a reason for everything you had a mind to do anyway).

Example 1 – Dan was in detention because he had been caught using his phone in the school library. He had been making a list of the pros and cons of asking a girl called Amie to go out with him. Having carefully completed his table he was caught when Amie saw the list and protested loudly because there were more negatives than positives. This display of spirit only attracted Dan to Amie more. Despite what the list said, he was using the detention to plan how he was going to persuade Amie to be his girlfriend.

Example 2 – Nanna was surprised to hear that the family had decided to go to Mallorca on holiday. She and her daughter had made a list of the benefits of Mallorca versus the week in Scotland which she preferred. Nanna was sure that Scotland had easily won, but despite its culture, shortbread, cool climate, and castles the rest of the family had chosen the Mediterranean island. Now Nanna had to decide whether to go with the family (they hadn't bought her a ticket in case she decided to stay at home).

Example 3 –

---

solutions are often arrived at through incompletely theorised agreements requires humility and honesty. Humility to admit we do not know why something works and honesty not to waste time gathering retrospective evidence to justify ourselves.

Working through incompletely theorised agreements also requires bravery. Too often, decisions are only questioned after outcomes become evident. Hindsight allows us to ignore the numerous possible outcomes of a decision at the time of its taking and only focus on the one outcome which came to pass, as if it were always inevitable. Alternative histories are lost from view, even though they may have been equally, or even more likely, to occur. In these circumstances, the urge to play safe and follow the expected path can be attractive. At least then, we can justify our decision.

Leaders need to be brave in asserting their problem-solving process and need to keep incompletely theorised agreements under review. The nimble, oblique approach ensures the team is ready to tack in a different, collectively agreed, direction as required. Problem-solving becomes a process rather than an act (Tilting the table 6.3).

The struggle to be brave

Being brave enough to follow incompletely theorised agreements through a process of successive limited comparison is hard in today's schools. Ever since the

Tilting the table 6.3 Incompletely theorised agreements

Incompletely theorised agreements are those decision which leaders take together without necessarily being able to offer a complete rational justification. Can you think of any incompletely theorised agreements which your school has in place in any of the following policy areas? How successful are these agreements in meeting a need?

Policy area	Description of incompletely theorised agreement	Success? (1= Highly Successful, 5= Why do we do it this way?)					Need for a review? Y/N
		1	2	3	4	5	
Homework							
Uniform							
Rewards							
Sanctions							
Staff well-being							
Attendance							
Pupil recruitment							
Community engagement							

marketisation process took hold in the 1980s, the status of the public sector has been downgraded and eroded. We are told that teachers are too remote from economic realities and market forces are needed to make public services more efficient. Targets, monitoring, and efficiency.

The public sector has gradually been gaslighted into believing that they are inferior and need to emulate rather than complement the private sector. Risk taking has been stifled because leaders are under pressure to minimise costs and scared of making mistakes. Teachers lack confidence and find innovation daunting.

Education can seem paralysed, second-guessing what answers we think are expected rather than confidently asserting our expertise and controlling the agenda. Yet the greatest British economist of the twentieth century, John Maynard Keynes, believed public services should not simply copy the private sector, but instead achieve goals that were fundamentally different.

Fundamentally different

The story of the discovery of penicillin is well known. An uncovered petri dish left by an open window grows mould in the same way that can be observed in staff room coffee cups up and down the country. By chance Alexander Fleming notices the mould has anti-bacterial properties and penicillin is discovered. Lucky Alexander Fleming. Except this was not luck. The conditions that created the mould occurred by chance, but to notice it and understand its significance required an expert. Fleming may not have fully understood what he was seeing but knew that it was important. 'Fortune favours the prepared mind' and Fleming had carried out years of research and experimentation to prepare his mind for this event.

In schools, as in laboratories, organised minds who are sensitive and responsive to change are essential. Trusting professionals who spend many hours in classrooms and around schools to follow their professional instincts; noticing and acting, in an iterative process of change and evolution that relies on expertise, openness, and risk taking. Perhaps this is the fundamentally different approach for which we should be looking.

Teaching is a vocation which needs the confidence to solve problems by developing and refining its own methods and strategies. Market forces have narrowed the focus too much. To broaden the view, we need to encourage leaders and teachers who are proud of working in an environment fundamentally and wonderfully different to the private sector. Complementing, but not enslaved to, the logic of efficiency, we need to step beyond half comprehended business strategies and develop something new and exciting. Let business learn from education.

Be aware (beware) of your brain

When it comes to solving problems, our brains are both our greatest asset and our greatest potential weakness. Built out of blood vessels and soft tissue and powered by glucose, brains have the processing power of multiple computers and contain the essence of our person. Evolutionary biologists and psychologists suggest that the lives of our early ancestors had a profound effect on the way our brains work today. In most cases these traits are beneficial, indeed essential, for our survival.

In his book 'Thinking Fast and Slow', Daniel Kahneman[36] identifies two different ways in which our brains operate. System 1 operates unconsciously, takes little energy, and is designed to keep things ticking over without draining our batteries too much. When we are in this passive, autopilot mode, the brain is still using up to about a quarter of all our energy. We only use System 2 thinking for those effortful mental activities which demand our full attention. Studies suggest that on average, people are capable of between 1 and 3 hours of fully active engagement per day before concentration wains. Our brains require astrocytic glycogen to make complex decisions which is replenished through diet, exercise, and sleep (another reason to look after our well-being).

The danger that lurks here is twofold. Firstly, our brains prefer to use System 1 because System 2 thinking is effortful, so we often fall into thinking errors first mentioned in Chapter 3. Secondly, we are largely ignorant of when we are using System 1. Our decision-making can be poor because our brains slip into lazy, thinking without us realising.

Knowing this, however, provides an opportunity. If we can devise solutions for our school which recognise, or even plan for, people's natural preference for lazy thinking, outcomes could be improved without altering the conscious decision-making process of anyone, staff or students. Maximum impact for minimum input.

Lazy thinking

Inertia can be difficult to recognise and overcome. In Physics, inertia describes the way that matter will continue in its existing state of rest, or movement in a straight line, unless that state is changed by an external force. In schools it is the tendency to do nothing or leave things unchanged.

Sometimes in schools, we have done things in a certain way for so long that we no longer remember why or recognise that it would be possible to change. Too much change can be bad but failing to change or question the prevailing state can mire schools in mediocrity. Better to carry out 'pre-mortems' on a regular basis. This means consciously scheduling time on a regular basis to consider the current state of things and whether they would benefit from an 'external force' for change (Tilting the table 6.4).

Tilting the table 6.4 Pre-mortems – If we can predict it, we can prevent it
Pre-mortems take place before issues arise and aim to pre-empt problems rather than looking back and attempting to identify causes with hindsight (post-mortem).

For each of the changes to policy, ask yourself what is the worst that can happen.

	Policy	Pre-mortem – What's the worst that could happen?	Is it worth doing?
Uniform	Allow students to wear trainers, provided they are entirely black with no logos.		
School day	Start 30 minutes earlier than currently, shorten the lunch break and finish 45 minutes before the current finish time.		
Homework	Stop issuing detentions for homework first and second offences and instead reward those students who complete all homeworks in a term.		

By failing to consider alternative futures we fail to recognise that doing nothing is itself an action. Carrying out a pre-mortem (rather than waiting for problems to arise and carrying out a 'post-mortem') enables the status quo to be assessed alongside its alternatives. It may be that the result is the choice to leave things as they are and that is a valid conclusion. However, failing to stress test current practice in this way enables our bias for the status quo to rule and stifles improvement.

Deciding to carry out a pre-mortem on seemingly settled aspects of practice without having a pre-conceived idea of an alternative can feel unsettling as a leader but will liberate ideas. At the least it will validate current approaches and at best it may uncover more efficient, exciting, and effective ways to do things.

Dangers of experience

Having argued elsewhere for the importance of recognising and harnessing professional experience it may seem paradoxical to warn against the fallibility of experience when looking for solutions. For example, people are far more likely to overestimate the chances of a risk occurring if they can readily call to mind examples of that risk occurring in the past, particularly if it involved a high level of trauma.

For example, in 2005 I had tickets to watch England play cricket against Australia at Lord's in London. I planned my journey carefully, however, on 7 July, four men detonated home-made bombs on different parts of London's transport system, causing mayhem, killing more than fifty people, and injuring hundreds. Two weeks later, having arrived in the capital on time, I made the decision to speed walk/jog to the ground rather than risk public transport. I arrived several minutes after the scheduled start and in a sweaty mess.

The reality was that I was in no more danger on London's underground that day than any day before or since but I overestimated the dangers due to recent events. In schools we might dismiss possible improvements because we have experienced passionate parental objections in the past, or continue costly but ineffective practices, because we have heard of how similar things have been tried in the past or turned out badly at other schools, perhaps being criticised during Ofsted inspections.

Sanctum syndrome

Understandably, leaders are expected to deal with students whose behaviour is of such a magnitude that main scale staff shouldn't have to deal with it. Figure 6.1 represents these behaviours in the top left-hand corner. Sanctions for these, most serious of transgressions, are dealt within the school's inner sanctums.

Many places of worship have traditionally had an inner sanctum. These are the most sacred parts of the temple and only the most important priests may enter. Those from the outer courtyards only enter the inner sanctum with fear and trepidation in the knowledge that they are to be judged by a superior power.

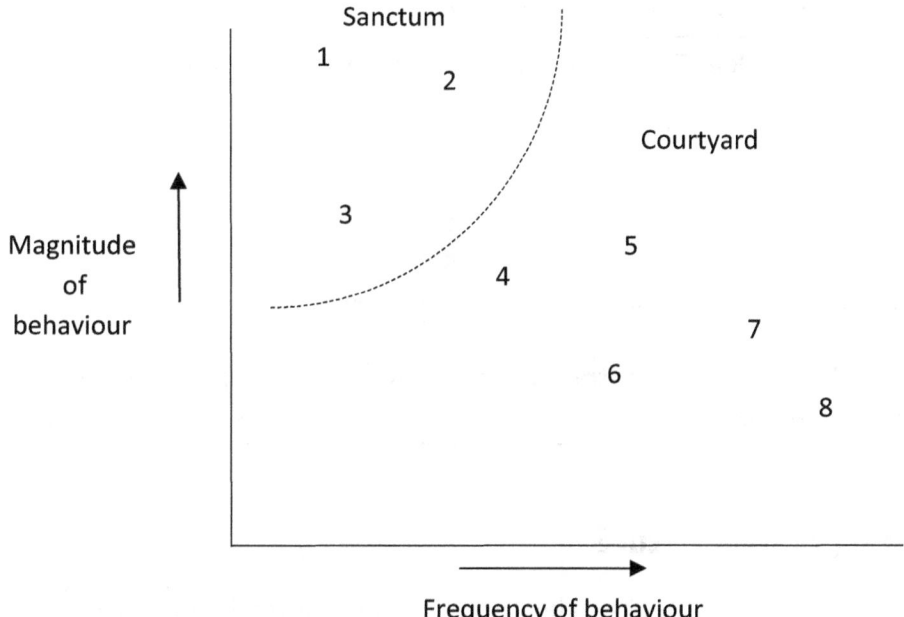

Figure 6.1 Sanctum syndrome

For students, the senior leaders' corridor, the head of year's office, or the head of department's classroom may be the equivalent of the inner sanctum. Being physically removed to this space can induce a heightened sense of anxiety which is itself a part of the reprimand process. It is rightfully part of the role of the school leader to help teachers manage behaviour in the wider school by presiding over the inner sanctum and judging those brought before them from the outside world.

However, if leaders' only role in discipline is to sit in judgement on referred extreme behaviours, it can create a distorted 'sanctum syndrome'. Leaders start to overestimate the chances of extreme behaviour and negative consequences because they experience them disproportionately and they can be traumatic, even for experienced senior staff.

If leaders only see the extreme behaviours, they may develop availability bias leading them to overestimate the prevalence of extreme behaviour. System 1 thinking can kick in and decisions be taken based on perception rather than reality. At best it may lead to a status quo mindset, attempting to stabilise a perceived delicate state of general behaviour. At worst, overly draconian, knee-jerk policies can transpire which antagonise the mass of students whose behaviour is within normal bounds but are less often experienced by leaders.

To avoid this it is important to plan to get out of our sanctums more often. Do more lunch and break duties, visit more classrooms, speak informally to more staff and students to get a more representative view of the true state of things (Tilting the table 6.5).

Tilting the table 6.5 What are the misbehaviours?

Have another look at Figure 6.1. What types of misbehaviour would you put as number 1 to 8?

1	5
2	6
3	7
4	8

Compare your list with a colleague – discuss any differences and see if you can reach a compromise list.

Can you think of any other strategies to reduce the build up of a sanctum syndrome amongst leaders?

Fighting human nature

People are natural optimists. When questioned about the lifetime possibilities of having a heart attack, developing a drinking problem or going through a divorce during their lifetime, students consistently underestimate the odds. Conversely, they significantly overestimate their chances of becoming a doctor, lawyer, or professional sports person.

Teachers are not exempt from this tendency. It seems reasonable to suppose that many beginning teachers significantly overestimate their abilities. This can lead to difficulties accepting critique unless professional development can achieve the tricky task of providing emotional support and realistic professional feedback. There are dangers if either approach starts to dominate.

New entrants to the profession will pick up messages about what a good teacher is from many different sources, mostly subliminal using their System 1 thinking because people tend to follow the herd when there are complex decisions to be made about behaviour. Our lazy brains will make an assessment about what most people do or think, judge that this conveys important information and act accordingly, simply following the herd, rather than reasoning things through for themselves.

Herd behaviour, coupled with the desire to fit-in created by unconscious peer pressure, create a collective conservatism in many school cultures that persists despite the transience of staff coming and going. If this goes unchecked, practices may be preserved for no better reason than 'its just the way we do things round here' rather than for any benefit, real or perceived.

Nudge, nudge: think, think

Advertising has been described as the act of selling people things they didn't know they wanted without them realising. Good adverts sell an aspiration which is attached to a product rather than the product itself. Advertising executives know how lazy our brains like to be and the world of possibilities this opens up to influence the way we think and act.

Think of all the indecipherable adverts for perfume which proliferate around Christmas time each year. To be fair to perfumiers it is hard to sell a product whose main virtue can only be experienced through the sense of smell, however the same principle applies to everything from food and drink to toilet cleaning products. We are told that we will be happier, more popular and/or more admired, and successful if we simply buy this detergent or that weed killer. Of course, the message is not spelled out to us. The advert simply implies this through visions of beautiful people and places and leaves our lazy brains to join the dots.

In the last fifteen years or so, governments have realised the potential for exploiting the biases our brains have developed for an easier life. In 2010, the coalition government formed a new organisation called the 'Behavioural Insights Team' whose job it is to make public services more cost effective and easier to use by exploiting a realistic view of human behaviour. In the intervening years they have, for example, sought to increase engagement with climate change initiatives, payment of taxes, youth voting rates, and the take up of private pensions. All of this merely by using 'nudges' to people's behaviour that enable them to make better choices for themselves.

Libertarian Paternalism

The authors of the best-selling book, 'Nudge',[37] Richard Thaler and Cass Sunstein, coined the term 'Libertarian Paternalism' to define the process of encouraging people to make better choices for themselves. 'Libertarian' because people should be free to make choices without forbidding options or offering economic incentives. 'Paternalism' because efforts should be made to steer people in the direction of choices that will improve their lives.

Making it easier to make the right choice leads to more people choosing well. In schools, people must make choices all the time. Which direction to walk, where to put litter, when to talk, where to play; daily life in schools consists of a never-ending procession of choices. Whenever people are asked to make a choice, how that decision is framed has a major impact on the choice made.

Nudging involves being conscious of the impact of how choices are framed on behaviour (also called 'choice architecture') and using this to the advantage of the individual and the community. It should be remembered that nudging cannot be avoided. Therefore, if we are solving a problem by asking people to make a choice, it makes sense to minimise the costs of making the right choice.

One of the first examples Thaler and Sunstein discuss in their book is a school cafeteria in which significant changes in the food chosen by students were made simply by rearranging the displays. This is well known by supermarkets, who influence shopper behaviour by placing the most profitable products at eye-level and piping in the smell of baking bread to encourage spending.

Humans are naturally lazy, and this is arguably even more the case for adolescents. This can be to our advantage. Students' tendency not to think things through is what presents us with the opportunity to nudge them into making better decisions without realising. People make poor choices when they are inexperienced, poorly informed and receiving feedback that is slow or infrequent. Students are, by their very nature, inexperienced and poorly informed – a key purpose of their schooling is to change this.[34]

What's more, the consequences of the poor choices they often make are almost always deferred. Failing to hand in homework tomorrow will result in poor exam grades in a few years' time. Dropping litter will result in an untidy and unclean environment for all in the future. Missing school or arriving late will reduce academic progress eventually but you get to enjoy a day in bed now, so who cares?

Schools traditionally favour commands, rules, and prohibitions to compensate for this. But nudge theory proposes that problems arise because students' minds are overly reliant on instinctive thinking. If we school leaders could manipulate this at a whole-school level, we could proactively reduce the number of poor choices that students make without having to resort to exhaustive lists of rules and increasingly stringent punishments: minimum input, maximum impact.

Nudging behaviour[38]

We know that young people are heavily influenced by the choices their peers make and the need to conform is strong. Emphasising that most students are doing the right thing is likely to nudge more students to follow their lead and fall into beneficial behaviour. For example, let them know explicitly that 92% of students are handing in their homework on time, or that 95% of students think you should tidy your lunch table after you've finished. This positive reinforcement is likely to become a self-fulfilling prophecy.

Indeed, people are so susceptible to suggestions that simply questioning someone's intentions (known as the mere-measurement effect) makes them more likely to act in a predictable way. Leaders can harness this by asking students what attendance they are aiming for or how many hours of revision they plan to do. Once the seed is planted, students are more likely to change behaviour to match their predictions, to their own benefit (Figure 6.2).

Advantage can be gained by making the unseen, seen. Abstract impacts of behaviour do not galvanise students to make changes. However, exemplifying the impact of seemingly inconsequential behaviours can shift thinking.

For example, let students know how many bags of rubbish are picked up on the school field each week, and how much of this could be re-cycled. This is likely to shift the social norm away from dropping litter.

Figure 6.2 Making the unseen, seen (1)

Placing images of eyes or smiley faces can shift behaviour significantly. In a shared kitchen area, displaying a photo of human eyes has been shown to increase the amount paid into an honesty box for coffee and tea[37]. The same principle lies behind the life-sized cardboard cut-outs of police officers used to reduce shoplifting. Do your own experiments with eyes and cut-outs in areas that you know are trouble spots for anti-social behaviours, but that are difficult to always monitor (Figure 6.3).

The example above is a PowerPoint slide which was updated and displayed weekly in a sixth form common room. Students reported increased motivation having seen how others in the year group were doing with their applications (note that the faces are anonymous, and the colours chosen were yellow and blue, rather than green and red, to remove any shaming effect).

Finally, displaying words associated with moods helps to establish those moods even when students are unaware of having read the signs. Try, for example, placing words such as 'happy', 'positive', and 'determined' on the walls in areas where students congregate, and experience shows that they will start to demonstrate more of these traits instinctively. Be careful, however, to change the words regularly to maximise impact. Our System 1 thinking is adept at filtering out information from our environment which has become predictable (Tilting the table 6.6).

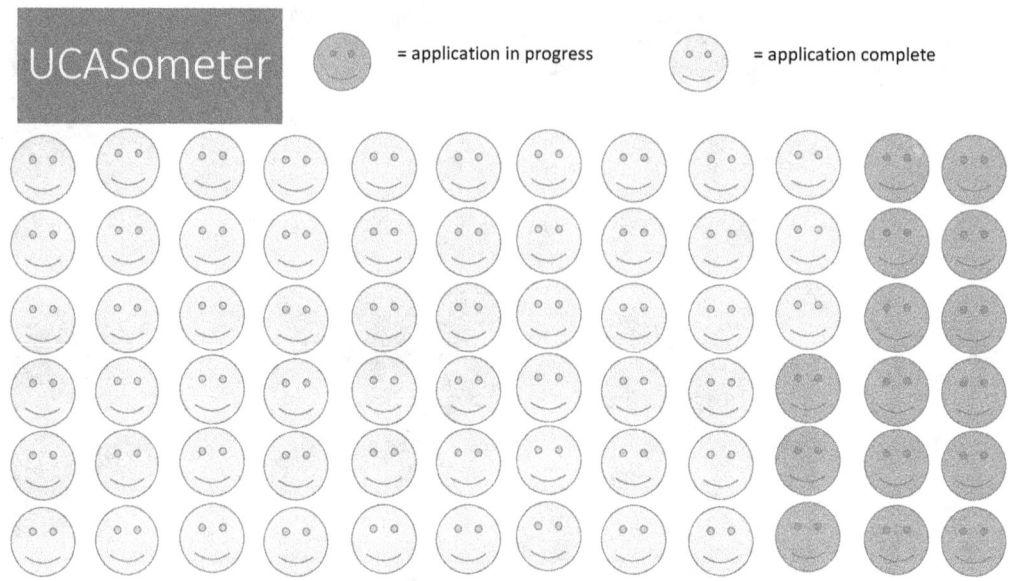

Figure 6.3 Making the unseen, seen (2)

Tilting the table 6.6 Fun with nudging

Think of some problems which have proved hard to solve in your school. Use the principles of nudging below to come up with some fresh thinking for solutions:

Herd behaviour	Students tend to follow the crowd – make them aware when the herd are moving in a 'positive' direction
Mere-measurement effect	Just asking someone about their intentions can increase the likelihood of action
Making abstract ideas real	Demonstrate concrete examples of the impact of poor decisions
Use of eyes and faces	Images of eyes and smiley faces can influence behaviour
Word displays	Displays of positive words can create positive behaviours

Cold decisions

In Homer's 'Odyssey', the hero, Odysseus, knows that his crew must sail close to an island inhabited by 'sirens'. These were beautiful creatures, half bird, and half woman, who lured sailors out of their boats with their beautiful song only to drown in the sea as they attempted to swim to shore. To protect his men, Odysseus commanded them to fill their ears with wax. However, to allow himself to hear the beautiful song, he instructed the crew to tie him securely to the ship's mast and not release him under any circumstances. When the siren song started, Odysseus struggled against the ropes and swore at his men to release him, but they stood firm and the hero survived.

Experienced teachers know that, like Odysseus, when students make choices in a 'cold state' they are more likely to switch to System 2 thinking and make positive choices. When students lose control, we know it is advisable to remove them from a crowd and give them thinking time before attempting discussion. This is not only true at the extremes. All students make thousands of instinctive choices a day. The more often they make these choices in a cold state, the better the quality of those decisions is likely to be.

Consider your school environment. Where are the places and when are the times when poor behaviour is most likely to occur? Think about your students who are most affected by sensory overload and least able to control their emotions. Use these students as your guides for a pre-mortem to anticipate which elements of the school increase the temperature at which students are making decisions. Ask to walk with them at break and lunch time and observe when they start to struggle.

You may find that simple strategies like clearing clutter from untidy surfaces and walls, clear signage and room numbering, floor coverings that absorb noise, and one-way systems to avoid bottlenecks will reduce distress for vulnerable youngsters. Not only this, however, they will also dial down the student temperature generally, so that more decisions are taken in a cold state and fewer bad choices lead to major repercussions.

Nudge justification

We cannot avoid the need to make decisions that will affect our young people, and they cannot always be informed of the thinking behind these decisions. Choices always need to be framed, so we have a duty to frame them in the manner that is most likely to create beneficial long-term choices for students. A judicious nudge in the right direction at the right time can reduce stress and increase success for students and staff.

However, you may feel uneasy about nudging student behaviour. Perhaps you feel it is too manipulative or duplicitous, particularly when we place such importance on openness and honesty as values. If this is you, I would encourage you to take the view of philosopher John Rawls and the ethics embodied by his 'Publicity Principle'. Simply stated, we should do nothing which we would not be prepared to defend to our community (students, parents, staff, and governors). To my mind, if this principle is respected, nudges are in the best interests of students and therefore justified.

Conclusions

- 'Big idea' thinking is seductive – we can be tempted to think that a new idea, if properly implemented for long enough, will be enough to solve a disproportionate number of problems.

- Direct problem solvers like to choose from a limited number of big ideas and then pursue these ideas doggedly, ensuring compliance across teams of staff.

- Committing to a big idea can lead to selective evidence and pursuing policies after they have ceased to be useful.

- Oblique problem solvers understand the limitations of their knowledge.

- Oblique problem solvers make an initial choice which they then keep under review in a process known as 'Successive Limited Comparison'.

- Although we like to think we make rational decisions based on appraisal of evidence (moral algebra) we often use this approach as a smokescreen to justify choices we have already made (Franklin's gambit).

- In reality, decisions are more usually made by 'Incompletely Theorised Agreement' – based on professional intuition and experience, as well as evidence.

- The dominance of the private sector generally has led to public sector workers (including teachers) to doubt their abilities and attempt to emulate instead what they think of as private sector values.

- A fundamentally different way of thinking in schools involves understanding the way people think and how this affects actions.

- Leaders need to beware of 'sanctum syndrome' which gives a distorted view of reality based on limited experience.

- It is easier to solve problems by nudging behaviour than by attempting to control it.

References

29 Lord, J.V., Burroway, J., Capaccio, G., and Moss, M., 1972. *The giant jam sandwich*. Houghton Mifflin.
30 Kay, J., 2011. *Obliquity: Why our goals are best achieved indirectly*. Profile Books.
31 Lindblom, C., 2018. *The science of "muddling through"* (pp. 31–40). Routledge.
32 Lumet, S., 2010. *Making movies* (p. 29). Vintage.
33 Schwartz, M.S., and Saiia, D., 2012. Should firms go "Beyond Profits"? Milton Friedman versus Broad CSR 1. *Business and Society Review*, 117(1), pp.1–31.
34 Wilson, T.D., Lisle, D.J., Schooler, J.W., Hodges, S.D., Klaaren, K.J., and LaFleur, S.J., 1993. Introspecting about reasons can reduce post-choice satisfaction. *Personality and Social Psychology Bulletin*, 19(3), pp.331–339.
35 Sunstein, C.R., 1994. Incompletely theorized agreements. *Harvard Law Review*, 108, p.1733.
36 Kahneman, D., 2011. *Thinking, fast and slow*. Macmillan.
37 Thaler, R.H., and Sunstein, C.R., 2009. *Nudge: Improving decisions about health, wealth, and happiness*. Penguin.
38 Clemmet, J., 2020. https://www.tes.com/magazine/teaching-learning/general/how-nudge-theory-can-help-students-make-better-choices

Tilting leadership

There are many contemporary leadership books today, which are best sellers and generate huge income. However, arguably one of the best quotes on leadership was written over 2000 years ago. The ancient Greek historian, Xenophon, described real leaders as being "loving and tough, straightforward and crafty, ready to gamble everything and wishing to have everything, generous and greedy, trusting and suspicious".[39] Despite their antiquity these words still ring true. Real leadership involves balancing contradictory approaches: love and toughness, honesty and craftiness, trust and suspicion. We all like simple solutions to complex problems, but real leadership is complicated.

Humans have long been beguiled by myths involving individual great leaders and their triumphs. From Alexander the Great to Greta Thunberg, we love to learn about exceptional people and what they achieve. However, the great leader model is ill-suited to modern schools. School leadership is a collaborative venture. The burden and joy of schools for all adults, is that our examples matter. For better or worse, the choices we all make, and the way we all behave, will influence and lead others.

Teacher and child psychologist, Haim Ginott, famously said;

> I've come to a frightening conclusion that I am the decisive element in the classroom. It's my personal approach that creates the climate. It's my daily mood that makes the weather... I can be a tool of torture or an instrument of inspiration. I can humiliate or heal.[40]

These inspirational words are not only true for teachers and children, but also for every adult who works in the school. We all have choices to make that will create the climate in our classrooms, corridors, and dining halls. The role of real leaders is to enable others, through our choices and example, to make the right choices more often.

This chapter will examine the facets of leadership which real leaders manage to balance. It will look at two distinctive types of leader, and ask you to reflect on your own leadership choices and what these tell you. We will consider how the

DOI: 10.4324/9781003241546-8

values leaders hold enable them to make fair and constructive judgements, bringing the best out of individuals and teams. The chapter concludes by considering the challenge of integrity under pressure. How can real leaders be successful in a 'post-truth' society without compromising their principles?

Hedgehogs and foxes

To become an effective leader involves mastering multiple leadership techniques. For the sake of simplicity, however, this chapter will adopt and adapt a model first proposed by the philosopher, Isiah Berlin. He categorised leaders as either 'Hedgehogs' or 'Foxes'.[41] We will flesh out these two extremes and consider the continuum of real leadership lying between them. Real leaders flex their approach as circumstances demand but will naturally gravitate towards one or the other. This chapter will consider the strengths and weaknesses of each approach, when they are most appropriate, which is most dominant in today's schools and whether there is a need to tilt this balance.

According to Berlin's model, hedgehog leaders are certain about their beliefs, and relentless in moving towards their goals. They are often highly regarded and provide reassurance in an uncertain world. Hedgehogs approach issues directly, deciding on a plan of action and doggedly pursuing it to its conclusion. There is no beating around the bush with a hedgehog leader and, like the real thing, they may become prickly if challenged.

Fox leaders, on the other hand, know how uncertain and volatile the world can be and are highly attuned to their environment. They are nimble in their thinking, adapting their strategies to changing circumstances. Foxes know that the world is complex and understand the limitations of their own knowledge. They prefer oblique approaches and are happy to change and run with instinctive solutions, even when imperfectly understood. Foxes know what makes people tick and tailor communication to their audience. Fox leaders may seem and unpredictable (Tilting the table 7.1).

Tilting the table 7.1 Hedgehog or fox? (1)

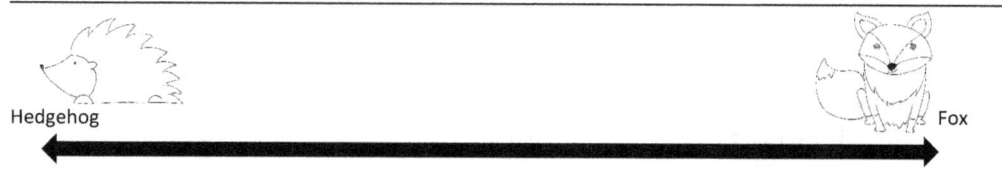

Hedgehog   Fox

From the limited amount you have learned so far, where would you place yourself on the hedgehog/fox continuum? Circle a number below.

Hedgehog									Fox	
1	2	3	4	5	6	7	8	9	10	

Leading in a crisis

Hedgehogs know that it is good for their reputation to succeed against the odds. It is easy to spot a leader in a crisis and hedgehogs are good at remaining calm and thinking clearly. Hedgehogs take charge and give instructions. People are relieved to have a hedgehog leader in difficult times and happy to follow their lead. Picture a football manager giving an inspirational half-time team talk or an officer rallying the troops before going into battle.

Foxes prefer to use their agile thinking to avoid a crisis. Imagine a health and safety inspector in the latter part of the last century who decided to make cockpit doors on passenger planes more secure. Or a civil servant in the 1990s who decided that UK schools should be fenced off from members of the public. In that alternative universe, 9/11 and the Dunblane shootings never happened. However, nobody would know the names of the individuals who avoided disaster. Foxes prefer to quietly improve the odds, and their contributions can therefore easily be missed.

To a hedgehog leader, the avoidance of disaster does not register as success. They are driven by outcomes that are tangible and quantified. In business they seek to maximise profits and shareholder returns. In schools, they want to be at the top of the performance tables. They are ambitious for their school and their students, so values and relationships can become subservient to results. They set clear, measurable plans and ensure compliance using rewards and inducements, surveillance, and sanctions. Hedgehog leaders are not afraid to make tough decisions and push through policies, even when they are painful. Under their leadership, however, a 'speed-camera culture' can develop in which staff perform as expected when being watched, and lapse into bad habits when unseen.

Fox leaders, on the other hand, understand that relationships really matter, and that sustainable success will only come when the web that connects teachers, support staff, students, and parents is healthy. It may flex under pressure, but the web will not break. Foxes constantly seek ways to strengthen bonds by building authentic professional relationships. They know that results are important, but it is shared values that drive sustainable improvement, shaping actions continuously and coherently across the complex and dynamic school environment. There is a danger that Foxes' aversion to conflict may mean honest conversations are avoided and schools become mired in happy mediocrity (Tilting the table 7.2).

Hedgehog leaders can thrive in the school environment. They are articulate and convincing about the perceived causes of their triumphs. They are confident in extolling the strengths of their approach and justifying actions they take in pursuit of success. Hedgehogs achieve a profile and standing which brings disproportionate influence.

But, like a good conductor, foxes know that the true sign of great leadership is when the leader goes unnoticed. The orchestra soars, but no one remembers the figure in the middle who controlled and directed through instinct and experience.

Tilting the table 7.2 Hedgehog or fox? (2)

Where would you place yourself now on the hedgehog/fox continuum? Circle a number below.

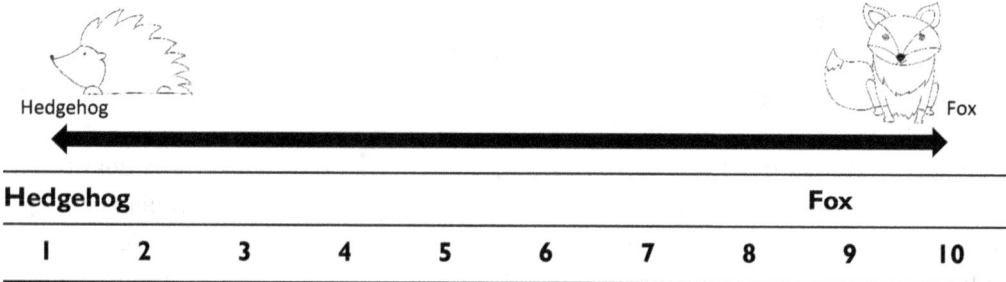

Hedgehog								Fox		
1	2	3	4	5	6	7	8	9	10	

Developing others

Decisions in schools are rarely between a right plan and a wrong plan. If we are lucky, the choice is between good and better, if not, between bad and less bad. In this situation, where multiple important decisions need to be taken each day across a school, the hedgehog leader's aura of certainty can rob staff of self-belief and cause paralysis. When faced with daunting moments, the hedgehog's team look to the centre and wait. People hedge their bets. Scared of failure, worried about the implications of innovating, they prefer to wait and be told what to do.

Although held in high-esteem, hedgehog leaders may simply be mistaken for great leaders because they survived when others of equal outlook and ability failed. People hang on their words and defer to their judgements. Hedgehogs understand that, with the power of hindsight, a clever hedgehog can always justify their decisions, regardless of the outcome, and emerge unscathed. If they lose their healthy fear of failure, hubris may follow. Leaders feeling empowered by the lack of challenge from others, become overly confident and make bad decisions.

Fox leaders, on the other hand, create a team ethos based on shared values that empower others to act. In a tight spot, all staff become real leaders who instinctively act together to avoid catastrophe. In complex environments, foxes have the confidence to leave others to make the right decisions. They make hundreds of small decisions every day that build the resilience of the organisation but remain largely hidden from view. Nobody waits, the school flexes and moves on. Because they prefer to remain in the shadows, it can be tricky to identify the precise contribution of a fox to success. Like a good football referee, all foxes instinctively know that if they are noticed, they are failing. Unfortunately, because of this, foxes may be overly diffident and struggle to articulate their strengths (Tilting the table 7.3).

Tilting the table 7.3 Hedgehog or fox? (3)

Direct (Hedgehog)	Oblique (Fox)
Believes in a master plan	Believes in continuous limited comparison
Actions justified by appeal to 'rational', evidence-based decisions	Actions informed by experience, evidence, and incompletely theorised agreements
Certain of beliefs	Understands the limitations of knowledge
Held in high regard – abilities overestimated	Abilities underestimated
Seeks to triumph against the odds – relishes a crisis	Seeks to reduce the odds – tries to avoid a crisis
Directs actions from the centre	Reinforces shared values from the centre
May becomes prickly if challenged	May seem inconsistent or manipulative (cunning)

For the final time, where would you place yourself on the hedgehog/fox continuum? Circle a number below.

Hedgehog					Fox				
1	2	3	4	5	6	7	8	9	10

Are there times when it is better to more hedgehog? Jot down some examples and explain them to a colleague.

Notes:

Are there times when it is better to be more fox? Jot down some examples and explain them to a colleague.

Notes:

Would a hedgehog or a fox be likely to perform better in an interview situation?

Notes:

What are the implications of this for your school's selection procedures?

The myth of the great leader

There is an understandable feeling that success is not accidental. It cannot be chance that a politician, business, or sports person triumphs. When we admire a champion, it is hard to accept that they might owe some of their success to luck. However, perhaps this could be the reality more often than we imagine.

There is a theory that if you gave typewriters to enough monkeys, and gave them enough time to type, eventually one of them would tap out the complete works of Shakespeare. This may be true in theory, but it would also result in a lot of broken typewriters. In addition, it would be a foolish publisher who offered the monkey playwright a contract for their next book. They may enjoy their moment in the spotlight, but sooner or later people would notice that the author was just a lucky monkey.

We naturally assume that high achieving head teachers and schools must be doing something right to achieve their eminence. It seems logical that if a school is successful, it must be caused by great leadership. This will sometimes, but not always, be right. This type of thinking (that if A follows B, B must have caused A), provides an example of what is called 'naïve empiricism'.

When we make repeated, empirical observations of events, people find it hard not to generalise about the causes of the event. If a monkey writes Shakespeare, it must be a genius. If a school, or subject in a school, does well it must be led well. These leaders are celebrated and promoted. However, for every monkey who produces legible text there will be millions who produce gibberish. In the same way, for every leader who succeeds there will be hundreds who made the same choices but failed.

If we make judgements based on good outcomes alone, rather than sound decisions, we should not be surprised when sometimes leaders are promoted beyond their competence. Leaders who were successful in one school (or business, or football club) fail to replicate that success elsewhere. Purely relying on outcomes and deducing excellence in reverse overlooks myriad other factors which contribute to success. It also promotes the dangerous myth of the great leader.

The halo effect

Napoleon is one of the most famous leaders in history. A brilliant and charismatic general, his influence lasted long after his death. But how much of his reputation as a military tactician is deserved is debatable. In a time before telecommunications, once a battle started, Napoleon would have had no way of knowing which of his orders were carried out or which were the most crucial moments of battle.[42] He saw victory as being achieved through his will, but in reality, randomness played at least as large a part.

The halo effect (or teleological fallacy) infers causes of events in reverse. It assumes that good (or bad) outcomes are caused by good (or bad) design. Napoleon won a battle, therefore he was a great general. This school performs well, therefore it must be well led. This subject underperformed; therefore, its leadership must be weak. The halo effect gives a comforting illusion of understanding events but is flawed.

For example, small difference in timing can cause changes in perception far out of proportion to any initial success. This 'first mover advantage' can calcify transitory advantage into accepted wisdom. The keyboard on which I am typing this text is a good example. Initially designed for manual typewriters, the letter positioning is designed to give maximum efficiency for punching keys without jamming the machine's mechanical arms. The QWERTY keyboard was ideal for the typewriter, but not for my laptop. An alternative DVORAK keyboard design has been shown to allow typing at significantly greater speeds, however, it is unlikely ever to take over from the universally accepted, but less efficient QWERTY version.

In school ecosystems, this first mover advantage has been amplified by the OFSTED policy of not inspecting schools deemed to be 'outstanding'. Once the outstanding label has been bestowed, social inertia ensures that schools can enjoy an extended period of unquestioned dominance without interference from inspectors. Even if parents are dissatisfied, they are likely to have sunk social costs. Having made a commitment to a school they practice self-deception, emphasising the positive and diminishing the downside. Not wanting to appear to have been mistaken, parents continue to support the school in the community, so a school's competitive advantage becomes entrenched. With intakes skewed towards proactive and engaged families, success becomes self-sustaining, despite but not because of the leaders of the school.

Check the mirrors but keep your eyes on the road

Travel writer, Robert Macfarlane, in his book 'The Old Ways', describes a terrifying car journey in the Himalayan Mountains of China which provides an interesting metaphor for naïve empiricism.

> Karim drove exceptionally dangerously, playing chicken with oncoming lorries and passing slower vehicles on the inside, bouncing along the rough verges of the road. Eventually, my heart thrumming as yet another lorry dopplered past, its horn blaring, I took to looking backwards, out over the hump of the spare wheel. There was never any trouble to be seen out of the rear window.[43]

The situation Macfarlane finds himself in illustrates the naivety of attempting to discern lessons about the future by studying the past. Looking out of the back window, all seems serene. It is easy to discern and admire the orderly scenery, pick out interesting landmarks, and draw comforting conclusions. However, this is a dangerous strategy.

Karim, the driver, justified his driving by reasoning that, as he had not yet been killed, he must be a great driver. But down the road is where danger lies, and the future is where leaders need to focus their attention. Too often, the accountability system in schools forces leaders to spend more time looking out of the back window and rationalising the receding view, rather than looking forward and preparing for what comes next. The ability of leaders to neatly describe and account for past outcomes is elevated above their instinct to look forward and respond to the varying challenges coming down the road. The unexpected, by its nature, is hard to anticipate so we should spend more time with our eyes on the road, using our mirrors only occasionally to check the rear view (Table 7.4).

Black swans[44]

My family and I once hired a holiday cottage in Ireland. On the last day, as we were doing a final sweep of the living room, an impressive, gilt-framed mirror fell to the

Tilting the table 7.4 Trouble ahead

In November 2007 the Cosco Busan, an enormous oil tanker, struck the Oakland Bay Bridge in San Francisco Bay spilling over 50,000 gallons of oil into the water and causing an environmental disaster and costing millions of dollars. The investigation found that the judgement of the maritime pilot, whose job was to guide the ship out of port, was severely impaired by the mixture of pharmaceuticals he had taken. Despite a pilot too spaced out to operate the electronic guidance systems, and sailing in thick fog, the captain of the ship failed to take action until it was too late and disaster truck.

A similar breakdown in communication is thought to have played a major role in the blocking of the Suez Canal, with global economic consequences in 2021, by the Ever Given container ship.

What obstacles is your team sailing towards which you need to speak up about before disaster strikes?

Obstacle	Timeline

floor with an enormous crash, smashing into hundreds of shards. Once I had established that no one was hurt, and we had tidied up the mess, I rang the landlord to explain what had happened. Since the mirror had been hanging on the wall for seven years without falling, in a classic example of naive empiricism, the landlord deduced that we must have been responsible for the mirror's destruction (and therefore liable for its replacement). Thankfully, the landlord eventually accepted our innocence, and our deposit was repaid.

Since antiquity the metaphor of a black swan had been used to denote something impossible. All sightings of swans confirmed that they were white feathered, therefore, if something was deemed as 'rare as a black swan' it meant it did not exist – a classic case of naïve empiricism. However, the meaning of the metaphor changed in 1697 when the first European explorers sailed into harbour in Western Australia and witnessed the native black swans for the first time. Now a black swan came to represent the fragility of knowledge derived from observation alone. Just because something has never happened before does not mean it will not occur in the future.

American writer, Nasssim Nicholas Taleb, defines back swan events firstly as being a surprise to the observer, secondly as having a major effect, and finally, after the event, appearing to have been predictable with the benefit of hindsight.[30] Karim did not expect to die behind the wheel because this had not already happened. My holiday landlord did not expect the mirror to fall because this had never happened. Schools that expect a past run of excellent results to continue into the future, without understanding the causes of their success, will eventually be disappointed. If we only look out of the back windscreen, we will never notice problems until they occur, by which time it will be too late.

The role of randomness

There is an apocryphal story from ancient times in which King Croesus, synonymous in the modern world with great riches, asked a visiting Greek philosopher, whether he is not truly the happiest man to ever have lived? Croesus was irked by the response. The philosopher replied that the happiest of men were those who went to their grave having lived a noble life and died in battle. When pressed, his explanation was that until we die there is always potential for our apparent good fortune to disappear. In such circumstances, definitive judgement should be reserved until one's end was known.

Circumspection is required in judging success. Philosopher, Karl Popper, defines great scientists as being men of bold ideas, but highly critical of their own ideas: "they try to find whether their ideas are right by trying first to find whether they are not perhaps wrong".[45] Likewise, real leaders are those who understand the limits of their own knowledge and experience. What seems right now is contingent upon circumstances and could change at any point. Leaders must be prepared to change to cope with what is coming down the road.

The certainty of a hedgehog leader may lend them a halo, but if success is purely based on outcomes these halos are illusory. It is necessary to have a plan, but a plan alone is not sufficient. When success is confidently attributed to the fulfilment of a narrow plan, without regard to the role of randomness, this is naïve empiricism. Like the monkey with the typewriter, the chances of success being repeated and sustained are small.

The allure of success

In Greek mythology, Achilles and Patroclus were brothers in arms during the Trojan wars, famous for their bravery and strength. Achilles had been dipped in the River Styx as a baby by his mother to ensure his invulnerability. His prowess and victories were legendary before he was finally killed when a stray arrow struck his heel (the ankle by which he had dangled above the river). But Achilles' best friend Patroclus was considered just as much a hero by the Greeks. So loyal was he to Achilles, that he disguised himself to take his friend's place in battle and was killed. Despite the heroic success of Achilles, and the military failure of Patroclus, both are celebrated heroes. One because of his success, and the other because of his character.

British history is also strewn with heroes whose motivations and character are celebrated despite, not because of, the results they achieved. Captain Scott died in the snowy wastes of Antarctica, George Mallory failed to conquer Mt. Everest (probably) and Tim Henman never won Wimbledon. Despite failure, these individuals are celebrated for their character and what they embodied, just as much as their achievements.

Today, however, it seems our culture has developed an unhelpful fascination with winners. As the ethics of the marketplace has pervaded society since the

1980s, there has been an increasing focus on success and successful people. Shows such as 'The Apprentice' reward greedy and selfish behaviour if it leads to success. Sports people earn millions with a 'win at all costs' mentality, even when this involves bending rules to breaking point. Politicians survive controversy and wrongdoing if they can spin the truth and standards of living are unaffected.

It can seem that success is all. Modern culture doesn't remember who finished second, let alone third, so ultimate effort goes into winning. When results are paramount, the temptation to succeed at any costs grows. At the same time, succeeding on your own terms or by different measures, is deemed as failure. This focus on success has had particularly profound effects on the way public services, including teaching, view themselves and are viewed by society.

Public bad, private good

Within economics, the traditional view is that the public sector should step in only when markets fail. Governments should provide services which the private sector would only partially provide such as water, electricity, education, and health. They should also step into enforce the rules if companies cheat; colluding to fix prices or exploiting their customers. However, even the governments' minimal role as carer and rule keeper was challenged by 'Public Choice Theory' in the 1980s.

Public Choice Theory challenged the competency of governments to provide and care for their citizens. Civil servants were portrayed as meddlers or do-gooders, and teachers as lazy and troublemaking. Governments were caricatured as being wasteful of public money, schools were inefficient, and teachers lacking in ambition and full of excuses. According to the prevailing narrative, only private companies could provide the modern, efficient, high-quality services that people deserved. Unnecessary government involvement became seen as the biggest barrier to progress across a range of services. A wave of privatisation followed designed to expose cosy public monopolies to the same economic imperatives that served the private sector so well.

Whatever the rights and wrongs of the economic debate, it has had a pernicious effect on the dominant mindset in public service. Even in a sector where mass privatisation is not possible, like education, the prevailing orthodoxy changed. If private businesses deliver the best and most efficient services but schools cannot be privatised, they at least should imitate the private sector to succeed. The predominance of versions of choice and competition, such as league tables and inspection judgements have gaslighted teachers and parents into believing that schools can only be good if the data says so.

Rather than being distinctive, public services strive to emulate private ones. Innovative school leaders can feel undervalued and frightened to make mistakes. Leaders are scared to take risks when they constantly feel scrutinised and judged by metrics over which they have no control. When, as a leader, you inhabit a society which believes you are second rate or part of a problem, this view can become internalised. Under these circumstances, it is hard for leaders in schools to develop

Tilting the table 7.5 Taking distinctive action

In the 1960s and 1970s Jaime Lerner was the mayor of the Brazilian city of Curitiba. He had big plans for creating a sustainable city and one of his first plans was to pedestrianise the downtown area. Local businesses were incensed and threatened court injunctions, but Lerner took the radical decision to complete a job, which should have taken 6 months, in 48 hours. Work began on Friday evening, after the courts had shut, and finished on Monday. "We had to work fast to avoid our own bureaucracy, and to avoid our own insecurity. So, the key issue in Curitiba was to start – we had the courage to start".[46]

We can be dissuaded from acting through fear of consequences, but often the anticipation of failure is worse than failure itself. Lerner assessed the cost of failure and took the risk, **using a distinctive approach to overcome the objections of the private sector**. In the event, the business owners profited greatly from the improved environment, dropped their opposition and Lerner went on to turn Curitiba into a city with a world-wide reputation for sustainable development.

Jaime Lerner, a public servant, had the courage to start –

1. Can you think of issues which have paralysed you in indecision? When have you waited, in deference to a more senior decision maker perhaps, and let an opportunity slip by?
2. Make a note of any problems you face currently, which you have put off addressing because they seem too daunting. Decide on a strategy and make a timeline to start and finish.

Issue	Strategy	Timeline

distinctive approaches and take actions which challenge, inspire, and build great schools (Tilting the table 7.5).

Ends and means

Our norms of behaviour should not depend on circumstances. If we understand the randomness of schools, we know not to take too much credit when things go well or assume too much responsibility for failure. The pressure of achieving results to satisfy external audiences, however, can undermine our beliefs and impede our decision-making. In the face of external pressures, it is only possible to maintain integrity if we are guided by shared values, but this is not easy.

Continuing with what we believe to be right, even in the face of opposition, is how leaders maintain dignity. Instead, however, it is easy to lose sight of values in the struggle to complete goals, carry out actions, and demonstrate success to others. Although we set goals to strengthen values, they can inspire actions which undermine and contradict. If righteous ends are used to justify nefarious means they destroy the values we want to nurture above all.

Tilting the table 7.6 Judgement by numbers

Read the extract below from 'The Every' by Dave Eggers.[47]
"A few months ago I went to see a movie without looking at the data beforehand and… afterward I walked out of the theatre thinking I really enjoyed it.…Then I got on my phone to look at the aggregate score, and it was a 44!"

Alessandro whistled mournfully.

"So then I had to adjust my thinking". Delaney said. "I mean how is it that I liked this movie that was a 44? Clearly I'd missed its flaws and inflated what I did like about it. By the next day, I'd thought it through enough and knew where I'd erred. It was definitely a 44. That's the last time I experience any kind of art before I have the numbers".

Numerical data and social media are widely used to judge everything from films to restaurants to schools. It is viewed as giving a more objective judgement of value than word of mouth, or even our own experience. As algorithms become more powerful, socially generated numerical data is likely to become more pervasive in making judgements within, and about, schools. What challenges does this create for leaders?
Notes

Leaders need the courage to meet with triumph and disaster and treat those two impostors the same.[48] Real leaders need encouragement to keep faith in what makes their school unique. This means judging others more on character and less on numbers. Decisions that turn out poorly should not be termed mistakes in hindsight. We need to hold others to account but give them freedom, encourage creativity but ensure consistency, inspire commitment but avoid burnout. Xenophon was right, leadership is complicated and contrary (Tilting the table 7.6).

Choice of truth

Now, more than ever, we live in a society which sees truth as being a relative term. Strong disapproval is still attached to lying, but in practice this means avoiding being caught in a lie rather than telling the straightforward truth. Using ambiguous language, selective use of data, and plausible deniability are all commonplace and unremarkable in wider society, and schools reflect society. Real temptation exists for leaders in schools to manipulate facts to create and enhance a narrative of success for the outside world.

There is a long history of leaders being economical with the truth. Tony Blair introduced 'spin doctors' to British government in the 1990s and former US Secretary of State, Henry Kissinger, coined the phrase, 'constructive ambiguity' during negotiations with the Chinese government in 1972. As long ago as 1875, in his novel, "The Way We live Now", Anthony Trollope's, Lord Nidderdale reflects that "… a few years ago a man could not have done such a thing… but that now it did not much matter what a man did – if only he were successful".[49]

Tilting the table 7.7 Truth or dare

Evan Davis, in his book *Post-truth: Why We Have Reached Peak Bullshit and What We Can Do About It*, draws the line of unacceptable truth manipulation as: "any communication that is not the clearest statement of the sincere and reasonable beliefs of the communicator".[50]

Think about the messages you communicate to students, staff and the wider community. Are you happy they meet Davis' definition?

Promotional material

School website

Self-evaluation documents

Other

On the sides of buses, and on posters at the gates, some schools have dived into self-promotion. However, the higher the stakes, the bigger the incentive to bend the truth. It is naïve to believe that schools do not manipulate facts. Performance data is complicated and dull, so some spin is unavoidable and this places schools in an ethical quandary. When communicating with a lay audience about value added, attainment, progress, and the rest, schools are forced to choose which truths to use and which to ignore (Tilting the table 7.7).

Dangerous messages

Whilst some degree of spin is inevitable, deliberate misrepresentation is dangerous. We cannot control who believes the stories we tell about ourselves. In 2015, VW became mired in a controversy which illustrates the point. In a bid to boost sales of its diesel models in the United States a huge marketing campaign had been launched focused on the environmental credentials of these cars. Unfortunately, the data on which the campaign was based had been fabricated. VW suffered huge financial and reputational damage from which it is yet to fully recover.

There was no deliberate plot by VW to cheat the public. The scandal happened because the company had such a focus on success and had invested so much in the green marketing campaign, that when faced with contradictory data, scientists chose to manipulate the figures and cheat rather than admit defeat. Nobody told them to, but a culture of competitiveness and fear led to workers telling their bosses what they thought they wanted to hear. If schools promote success focused purely on outcome measures, it should not be a surprise if teachers also cut corners and report what they think is expected rather than the truth.

There is not always time in busy schools to tell the whole truth and people are often tired or emotionally fragile, so plain speaking may be dangerous. In such circumstances selective use of truth, euphemism, and courtesy are understandable and acceptable tools to shape appropriate messages. However, the real leadership challenge is creating a culture which encourages honest communication. Such a culture must be kind enough to offer support, aspirational enough to encourage challenge and supportive enough to facilitate change. Let us finally consider the practical approaches taken by real leaders to grow such a culture in schools.

The paradox of authenticity

Authenticity is one of the most important facets of leadership at all levels. Leaders need to be natural and show their humanity. But planning to be natural seems contradictory. The seeming paradox is resolved when one considers what authentic behaviour looks like. It is not about oversharing personal information or deliberate demonstrations of affection. It is honesty about what you find difficult and integrity in demonstrating consistent behaviour, regardless of circumstances, that is aligned with one's professed values. People need to know what you stand for and that this does not change with the weather.

Authenticity should not be confused with charisma. Charisma can be an asset but is not a necessary component of real leadership. Furthermore, if unchecked, it can easily tip over into over-confidence and hubris, courting disaster and alienating others. While it is important not to seek affection, neither is it helpful to make a virtue of aloofness. Effective leadership requires the exercise of patience, empathy, resolve, self-discipline, and determination. Authenticity lies in admitting weaknesses but continuing to exercise. As with any exercise, repetition improves performance.

A proverb suggests that we all consist of three distinct people. The person we think we are, the person others think we are and the person we are. We may not think ourselves authoritarian, for example, but be thought of as such by others. Maybe we aim to inspire others to greatness and, but only seem to inspire grudging compliance. We cannot control the way that others view us, so what matters is knowing the person we think we are and want to be. The truth is somewhere in the middle. As always, balance is the key.

The wisdom of experience

Over time leaders develop invaluable experience which hones their skills and nurtures their intuition. Things seem to come naturally to the outside eye. This can blind new leaders to the years of practice and struggle which led to the seemingly effortless actions of the experienced leader. Expecting new leaders to develop and mature purely through proximity with experienced leaders is flawed thinking. However, it can also be counterproductive to burden potential leaders with too much theory, causing over-thinking and stilting authenticity. It should be part of the role of leaders to widen the thinking and boost the confidence of those who will emulate and perhaps surpass them one day.

One area which can be daunting to novice leaders is running meetings with strong characters who may hold many years of experience. When nervous, the dangers are to become too doctrinaire at one extreme or laissez-faire at the other. Knowing when to consult and when to dictate is crucial. Team decision-making is often about throwing ideas around, and steering conversation until ideas appear to emerge organically. This is unlikely to be a bland process; lively and occasionally inharmonious exchanges are to be expected. Provided respect is maintained, and no one voice dominates, such interplay should be welcomed. After all, consultation is not just about sharing information, it is also a means to shape the group dynamic, building trust and relationships.

The constituents of great leadership continue to be elusive, 2000 years after Xenophon. Ultimately the greatest asset a leader has is their interest in, even fascination with, people. What makes them tick? Why they behave as they do and what barriers prevent them meeting their potential? Only if a leader has this authentic interest can they start to remove impediments and create the organic web of leadership that gives a school resilience. Sustainable success does not rest on one 'great leader' but rather is built on a leadership mindset that permeates all staff.

Leadership for all, by all

From the mid-day supervisor to the head teacher, all adults are role models for students and staff. We all play a role in delivering great leadership through the choices we make and the behaviours we exhibit. The only mark great leaders have in common is that people choose to follow them. Even when it would be easier not to, they follow.

Elevating individual leaders to the level of greatness based on outcomes alone is wrong. It causes paralysis while people wait before daring to act. It also gaslights good potential leaders into thinking that only a select few, exceptional individuals can become great leaders. In addition, the success of unethical leaders disheartens, and may corrupt, ambitious novice leaders looking for role models. Finally, it rewards those who are willing to act unscrupulously in single-minded pursuit of measurable outcomes.

Every adult in a school plays a vital role in the web of leadership. They can and should be shown how to improve as leaders. Leadership is not about hierarchy but about mindset. It is not something people do to each other but something we do for each other. We need to be united by shared values, to think independently and learn together; tilting education in a new direction that judges success as much by values as by outcomes (Tilting the table 7.8).

Tilting the table 7.8 Your non-negotiables

Choose your top five attributes of real leadership. Compare your list to someone else's list and discuss/explain any similarities and differences.

Empathic	Direct	Fox	Creative
Hedgehog	Value driven	Humble	Kind
Authentic	Decisive	Oblique	Patient
Self-disciplined	Intuitive	Resolute	Certain
Well planned	Persuasive	Fair	Outcome driven
Other	Other	Other	Other

Conclusions

- Real leadership is about balancing complex, and sometimes conflicting, aims.

- In order to analyse leadership, it can be useful to use a simplified model, such as the hedgehog vs. fox continuum.

- Hedgehog leaders are direct and certain of their plans but may become prickly when challenged.

- Fox leaders are oblique, aware of the limits of their knowledge, and run the risk of seeming uncertain or manipulative.

- Having a 'great leader' view of school leadership is unhelpful. It undermines the resilience of a school and fails to develop novice leaders.

- There are many reasons why some leaders, schools, or departments succeed – in complex environments, chance plays a significant role.

- Once perceived success has been achieved, social inertia means the perception remains, even though the performance may not.

- Modern society loves a winner. This may encourage a 'succeed at all costs mentality'.

- Modern society treats truth as relative, creating temptations for leaders to manipulate the truth unscrupulously.

- In the face of uncertainty, the only way to preserve dignity is to maintain values and behave consistently.

- Leadership is about a mindset, not a hierarchy – successful schools nurture leadership at all levels through a culture of kindness, aspiration, and support for all.

References

39 Brearley, M., 2015. *The art of captaincy*. Pan Macmillan.
40 Ginott, H., 2009. They said it first.... *Phi Delta Kappan*, 91(4).
41 Cuban, L., 1995. Hedgehogs and foxes among educational researchers. *The Journal of Educational Research*, 89(1).
42 Kay, J., 2012. Obliquity. *Capitalism and Society*, 7(1).
43 Macfarlane, R., 2012. *The old ways: A journey on foot* (Vol. 3). Penguin.
44 Eggers, D., 2021. *The Every: A Novel*. Vintage.
45 Davis, E., 2017. *Post-truth: Why we have reached peak bullshit and what we can do about it*. Little, Brown Book Group.
46 Taleb, N.N., 2007. *The black swan: The impact of the highly improbable* (Vol. 2). Random House.

47 Kipling, R., 1910. *If. From "Rewards and Fairies."* Garden City, New York.
48 Taleb, N.N. and Raju, P.V.L., 2011. *Fooled by randomness.*
49 Trollope, A., 2005. *The way we live now.* Broadview Press.
50 https://www.theguardian.com/cities/2016/may/06/story-of-cities-37-mayor-jaime-lerner-curitiba-brazil-green-capital-global-icon

Conclusion

Shifting the window

American political analyst, Joseph P. Overton, proposed that within the political system there were a spectrum of ideas and policies which lay within a 'window' of acceptability[51] (Figure 8.1). Ideas which lie within the window are uncontroversial and debated within mainstream dialogue. Political discourse is contested within this range, but ideas lying beyond the window are considered extreme and dismissed.

For example, school inspection frameworks which take staff workload into account or specify the importance of mental health in the curriculum are important and lie within the current Overton window for education. Limited change, and within acceptable limits. However, as long as the inspection framework also includes high-stakes judgements, stress levels for staff and children will remain damagingly high, blighting the learning of generations. If we seriously wish to address these problems, we need to tilt education and shift the Overton window.

Lessons from the land

Farming provides some interesting parallels to schooling in the UK. Much of modern farming is driven by the market, minimising costs and maximising revenues to provide the best returns for shareholders. A relatively small number of massive multi-national corporations own vast expanses of farmland. They invest large sums to increase yield and drive down costs. Unfortunately, because environmental harm does not appear on a spreadsheet and human costs are not factored in, water is polluted, soils exhausted, and people damaged by the system.

From the 1960s onwards, farms across Europe were incentivised to grow crops by guarantees of minimum prices for the food they produced. With no downside to over production, farmers bought more land into cultivation and applied more intensive

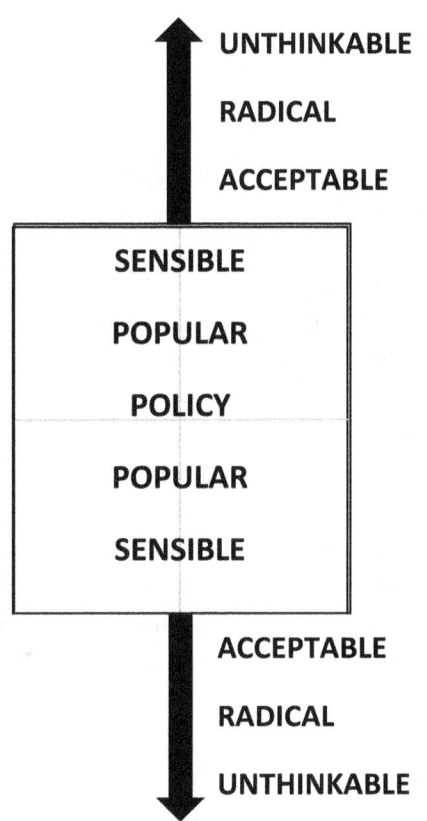

Figure 8.1 Overton's window

inputs to maximise yields. Multi-nationals bought out smaller farmers and made huge profits. The result was huge gluts of everything from wine and milk to butter. At the same time, natural habitats disappeared, replaced by soulless monocultures and damaging chemicals caused natural populations of many wild species to plummet.

The damage caused has now been recognised. Shifts in public opinion, and consumption patterns, have worked together to shift the Overton window. Ideas which formerly lay outside the mainstream, such as organic farming or paying farmers not to farm but return land to nature, have become accepted government policy in an effort to protect what is important to us about the countryside.

The education and agriculture systems are both efficient in delivering their aims. As consumers, we cannot avoid being complicit in either process. Like farming, intensive education is driven by market forces although it uses proxy measures to replace profit as a measure of success. Also, like farming, certain costs are not factored in. Staff and student well-being, for example, are not included within proxy measures so are not counted as a cost of achieving success. In farming, the damage was done to the soil and wildlife, in education it is seen in staff and students struggling to work longer hours, more intensively.

Challenges for schools

Schools have driven up standards but often at the cost of anxiety and the loss of joy from education. Learning has become more a process of measurement and assessment than relationship and enlightenment. The metrics for judging success are complex and confusing for non-specialists, leaving the field open for unscrupulous schools to take advantage with slick marketing. The system limits the number of schools which can be considered 'above average' making parental choice an illusion and creating inertia. The 'best' teachers and students gravitate to a small number of what are known as 'outstanding' schools in what becomes a self-sustaining hierarchy.

With schools in competition with each other, collaboration is stifled, and overburdened leaders can be forgiven for desperately grabbing at the next big idea in a kind of educational kleptocracy. Without time to develop thinking in depth, ideas are adopted wholescale without sufficient adaptation, sustaining a mediocre merry-go round of half understood and quickly forgotten innovations. Great ideas struggle to spread across the system, and a small number of skilful self-promoters can gain disproportionate influence. Without a shift in the educational Overton window, things will not get better.

Solutions for schools

This is being written in the spring of 2022 when the world seems to have changed dramatically. Climate change, the global pandemic and war in Ukraine have provided clear evidence of the fragility of the long period of consensus which had dominated Western politics, economics, and education for the previous thirty years. Education has a responsibility to ask questions of itself at such times. This book has argued that education should not simply respond to and imitate dominant values, but shape those values.

Many of us have become so familiar with the way that our schools are incentivised and judged that we have stopped noticing. League tables, Ofsted ratings, and the rest are so entrenched that it is hard to see a different way of doing things. But education is too important not to at least try. Without a wider debate and questioning of the current accountability systems, innovation outside the window of acceptability will remain difficult to achieve.

Perhaps we can learn from farming and introduce a certification system. Farms who wish to become organic must go through a process at the end of which they are certified. Provided they continue with their processes they retain their organic status. Schools too could aim to demonstrate their worth by attaining a certification status. Certification could depend equally on academic outcomes, processes to promote kindness amongst staff and students, evidence of the self-reliance of learners, environmental sustainability, and financial stewardship. Provided schools have the processes in place to meet these goals they retain their certification. No judgemental and misleadingly definitive labels, just the confirmation that children are receiving the best education possible in that community.

The virtue of being good

Leaders in education, at all levels, have the opportunity and responsibility to help the next generation of leaders shape their thinking. More of the same is not an option, unless we are happy to continue with schools riddled with student anxiety and staff burnout. This book has tried to set out alternatives.

The chapters, which have focused on values, models, evidence, teams, commitment, problems, and leadership, are designed to tilt education with practical suggestions that would bring about a quiet revolution. One which believes that not everything that matters can be measured and not everything that can be measured matters. However, the single biggest change leaders in schools can make is to embrace the virtue of being good.

An obsession with the 'Outstanding' label from Ofsted can drive leaders to take actions which contradict the values they are supposed to support. The myth that being outstanding means meeting the needs of children and staff in the best way possible needs to be debunked. Being brave enough to say that 'Good' is good enough, immediately alleviates perverse incentives which drain students and staff freeing them to take risks and thrive.

What now?

Overton's theory suggests that policy makers will only adopt ideas within the acceptable range. To expand the window for education requires those with novel ideas to persuade others of their acceptability. That has been the aim of this book. Encouraging you to think independently and discuss your ideas with others so that we learn together. This is the essence of 'Tilting Education'. Changing mindsets to alter the direction of travel for education and producing high achieving, healthy, and ethical learners who will ask questions and actively shape a just and kinder future for themselves.

I hope you have enjoyed reading this book. The intention was to get teachers thinking, exchanging ideas, and trying new approaches. Some of the ideas may seem extreme to you, but this book is written in the spirit that "… the greatest madness is to see life as it is rather than what it could be".[52]

All of the 'Tilting the Table' activities are available to download for free from the Tilt Education website (www.tilt-ed.org) so go ahead and start real change in your school.

References

51 Cameron, W.B., 1963. *Informal sociology: A casual introduction to sociological thinking* (Vol. 21). Random house.
52 Miguel de Cervantes Saavedra. https://www.theguardian.com/books/2008/jun/10/miguelcervantes#:~:text=%22When%20life%20itself%20seems%20lunatic,not%20as%20it%20should%20be.%22

Bibliography

One book leads to another. These are the books which made up the chain which led to the book you are holding.

Brearley, M., 2015. *The art of captaincy*. Pan Macmillan.
Bregman, R., 2018. *Utopia for realists*. Bloomsbury Publishing.
Davis, E., 2017. *Post-truth: Why we have reached peak bullshit and what we can do about it*. Little, Brown Book Group.
Harari, Y.N., 2014. *Sapiens: A brief history of humankind*. Random House.
Kahneman, D., 2011. *Thinking, fast and slow*. Macmillan.
Kay, J., 2012. *Obliquity: Why our goals are best achieved indirectly*. Profile Books.
King, S., 2000. *On writing: A memoir of the craft*. Simon and Schuster.
Klein, N., 2007. *The shock doctrine: The rise of disaster capitalism*. Macmillan.
Lumet, S., 2010. *Making movies*. Vintage.
Macfarlane, R., 2012. *The old ways: A journey on foot* (Vol. 3). Penguin.
Mazzucato, M., 2018. *The value of everything: Making and taking in the global economy*. Hachette UK.
Mohamed, H., 2020. *People like us: What it takes to make it in modern Britain*. Profile Books.
Ngugi wa Thiong'o, 2007. *Wizard of the crow*. Random House.
O'Brien, T., 2015. *Inner story: Understand your mind, change your world*. CreateSpace Independent Publishing Platform.
Raworth, K., 2017. *Doughnut economics: Seven ways to think like a 21st-century economist*. Chelsea Green Publishing.
Smith, E., 2012. *Luck: What it means and why it matters*. A&C Black.
Syed, M., 2019. *Rebel ideas: The power of diverse thinking*. Hachette UK.
Taleb, N.N., 2005. *Fooled by randomness: The hidden role of chance in life and in the markets* (Vol. 1). Random House Trade Paperbacks.
Taleb, N.N., 2007. *The black swan: The impact of the highly improbable* (Vol. 2). Random house.
Thaler, R., and Sunstein, C., 2009. *Nudge: Improving decisions about health, wealth, and happiness*. Penguin; 1st edition.

Index

Note: **Bold** page numbers refer to tables; *italic* page numbers refer to figures

Achilles 113
Antiques Roadshow 10
arousal 79–81, **80,** 85
attribution bias **47,** 48–49
authenticity 118
availability bias 97

Berlin, Isiah 106
binary thinking 2, 28, 29, 34, **52**
Black Swans 111–112
bogus quantification 81
brain writing 63
British museum 19
Burnley FC 11

ceilings and floors 30–31, *33*
clone team *61,* 61–62, 71, *72,* 73
commitment and motivation 73–74, *75,* 81
complexity 25–26, 41–42, 60, 76
constructive ambiguity 116
Cosco Busan **112**
Croesus 113
csikszentmihalyi, mihaly 78
curve (The) 20–24, *21,* 33

Davis, Evan **117**
deference 40, 62–63, **115**
direct problem solving 89, 104, 109, 120
division of labour 55, *56*
dominance hierarchy 2, 26, 62, 62, 67–68, 104

doughnut model 18, 29–34, *32*
drone view 84
Dunbar's number 45

educational kleptocracy 124
Eggers, Dave **116**
empathy 75, 84–85
epoché 75–76, 76, 84–85, 85

feedback 62–63, 77–78, **79,** 83, 98, 100
first mover advantage 110–111
Fleming, Alexander 93
floors and ceilings 30–31, *33*
flow 78–80, **80,** 85, *85*
fox 106–108, **106, 107, 109,** 119, **120**
Franklin's gambit 90–91, **92,** 104

GDP 20–21
Ginott, Haim 105
Goodhart's Law 41–42, 44

halo effect 110
hedgehogs 106–108, **106, 107, 109,** 119, **120**
Herzberg, Frederick 73, **74**
hindsight bias 46
Homer 102
homophily 57–58, 60, 63
honest conversations 77, 107

imagined realities 18
incommensurate goals 26, **27,** 29

incompletely theorised agreements 91–92, **93**, 104, **109**
inertia 3, 95, 111, 120, 124
intuition 91, 104, 118
inverse skills problem 35, 52, 66–67
I-shaped leaders 64, *64*

Jotham's story 6

Kahneman, Daniel 94
Kelvin, (Lord) 38
Keynes, John Maynard 93
Kissinger, Henry 116
knowledge clustering 58

league tables 2, 23, 39, 114, 124
Lerner, Jaime 115
Libertarian Paternalism 99
Liverpool FC 11
loss aversion **47**, 49

Macfarlane, Robert 111
marketisation 2, 11, 13, 23, 92
Maslow's hierarchy 80, *81*
maths anxiety 36
maximisation 11, 16, 122
mere-measurement effect 100
meritocratic recruitment 58
modernism 87
monkeys with typewriters 110, 113
moral algebra 91, **92**, 104
motivation and commitment 73–74, *75*, 81

Napoleon 110
nudge 98–100, 103

obliquity 89–90, 92, 104, 106, **109**, 120, **120**
Odysseus 102–103
Ofsted 10, 13–14, 40, 43, **47**, **62**, 89, 96, 111, 124, 125
optimistic future view 15, *15*
Overton, Joseph 122–125, *123*

Paddington 35
Paradox of Praise **47**, 50
personal values 4–5, **5**, 8, 15–16

perspective blindness 57, 68
pessimistic future view *15*
pin factory 55
Popper, Karl 113
pre-mortems 95–96, **95**, 103
Prestige Hierarchy 62–63, 68
principals and agents 40–42, **42**, 52
'Progress 8' 11, 22, **39**
proxy measures 10–12, **12**, 123
public choice theory 114

quantitative revolution 38–39, 51

randomness **52**, 68, 110, 113, 115
rational decision making 91, **92**
Rawls, John 103
Raworth, Kate 26

sanctum syndrome 96–98, *97*
shared values 7–10, **8**, 14–19, 28, 33–35, 40, 43–44, 57–60, 72, 90–91, 107–108, **109**, 115, 119
SMART-IE targets 35, 43, 52
Smith, Adam 55
spinning the truth 114, 116–117
Successive Limited Comparison 89, 92, 104
Sunstein, Cass 91, 99
superhero leaders 66–69
survivors' bias 68
symbols 19–20, **20**, 25
synthetic quantification 37–38
System 1 and System 2 thinking 94, 97–98, 101

Taleb, Nassim Nicholas 112
teleological fallacy 110
Thaler, Richard 99
TILT teams 60, 68, 71, *72*, 76, 85
Trollope, Anthony 116
T-shaped leaders 63, *64*, 66, **67**, 69

unintended consequences 22–23, 29–30, 41

volatility **47**, 49–50

Xenophon 105, 116, 119

For Product Safety Concerns and Information please contact our EU representative GPSR@taylorandfrancis.com
Taylor & Francis Verlag GmbH, Kaufingerstraße 24, 80331 München, Germany

www.ingramcontent.com/pod-product-compliance
Lightning Source LLC
Chambersburg PA
CBHW080225170426
43192CB00015B/2755